Disclaimer

The information provided in this book is designed to provide helpful information on the subjects discussed. This book is not meant to be used, nor should it be used, to diagnose or treat any medical condition. For diagnosis or treatment of any medical problem, consult your own physician. The publisher and author are not responsible for any specific health or allergy needs that may require medical supervision and are not liable for any damages or negative consequences from any treatment, action, application or preparation, to any person reading or following the information in this book. Any references included are provided for informational purposes only. Readers should be aware that any websites or links listed in this book may change.

Perennial Gardening

Easy To Follow Guide
Plant Once And Enjoy Your Plants, Flowers, Shrubbery and Vegetables Forever

By Susan Hollister

Table of Contents

CHAPTER 3: GRASSES, SHRUBS, AND FOLIAGE PLANTS

CHAPTER 4: PERENNIAL BULBS AND RHIZOMES 64

Introduction

I want to thank you and congratulate you for getting this book. In the vast world of gardening, you encounter all sorts of plants. While annuals and biennials are common, the long-lived perennial is the focus of this book. Perennials usually develop during the spring and summer, die back during the fall to lie dormant all winter, and then reappear the following spring. These plants are popular, because their nearly limitless durability makes them easy to plant, maintain, and endlessly admire.

This book will help you discover a whole world of perennials you can introduce into your yard to enhance its beauty. Some have a limited blooming season, while others produce colorful flowers all summer long. Perennials even include certain vegetables, in addition to the ferns, shrubs, herbs, bulbs, fruits, grasses, and flowering plants we'll cover in this book.

In regions where the climate is mild, many perennials grow year-round. In climates where perennials are limited to growing during a few weeks or months, they will die down and sink into dormancy until the next growing season begins. Evergreen perennials, on the other hand, keep their foliage all year, regardless of where they grow.

Some perennials require a couple years to settle in before they begin to produce flowers, while other start blooming the same year they are planted. A whole group of perennials contains rhizomes or tubers, energy-housing root structures that enable them to survive the winter and continue to sprout and bloom year after year. We'll discuss the unique requirements of each type of plant and set you up to enjoy them for years to come.

You will also discover how to use perennials for therapeutic purposes. Some plants can improve your overall mood, sharpening your attentiveness, and even healing some illnesses. Lavender, for example, is a beautiful addition to any garden, but it has qualities that help relax and refresh the mind.

You will also learn how to use perennial plants to address landscape challenges. The roots of perennials allow them to survive not only harsh temperature extremes but also wildfires. You can take advantage of perennials' root systems to protect the ground from soil erosion. Perennials can also minimize groundwater contamination and prevent weed overgrowth. The hardiness of these long-lived plants reduces the need for herbicides and insecticides, because they tend to be naturally resistant to pests and disease.

Perennials can be found in backyard gardens, therapeutic gardens or as part of landscaping efforts that can range from privacy screens and borders to dramatic features. The plants themselves often cost more than annuals, but for this one-time investment, you get years of growing, blooming, delight!

Perennial gardening calls for more advanced planning than working with annuals. Once you have planted a perennial, you're pretty much stuck with it in that location for the life of the plant. However, with the tips and information provided in this book, you can be confident that your perennials will thrive and you will love where they're planted. I walk you through each aspect of planning the placement as well as the care and feeding of each perennial in your yard.

This book contains proven steps and strategies on how to properly design a perennial garden and to sustain thriving perennial displays on your property. You will learn about flowering perennials, grasses and shrubs, bulbs, herbs, and other plants used for landscaping. You will also receive valuable advice on arranging your plantings for the best visual advantage.

A description of each plant is followed with step-by-step instructions on proper growth and care. I have included tips that will help you know where each plant will grow at its very best and how to group specific plants for both the greatest visual impact and to honor symbiotic properties of each plant. Let's get started.

Chapter 1: Vegetables As Perennials

Although only a handful of vegetables grow as perennials, there are many reasons you should include some of them in your vegetable garden. Not only do they come back year after year with minimal maintenance, but they are often virtually indestructible and can serve as beautiful, yet edible landscaping for your property.

There are seemingly endless benefits to including perennial vegetables in your garden. In addition to providing beautiful landscaping, they can help prevent soil erosion. Some perennials produce their own fertilizer. Many introduce nutrients into the soil that are needed by other plants. They can attract beneficial insects and taller plants can provide shade for sun-sensitive varieties.

Of course, there are a few disadvantages to perennial vegetables. Many are slow growing, so it can take a couple years to become established enough to produce anything you can eat. Some perennial vegetables have strong flavors that are unfamiliar to American gardeners. Some must be harvested early to prevent them from tasting bitter and while most perennials are low maintenance, if you ignore them entirely, some can become quite invasive.

This may sound obvious, but perennials take a little more planning than annuals. Once you pick a spot for these plants, they will continue to grow there year after year, so it makes sense to have a general idea where you want them to reside on your property.

Here are some perennial vegetables, along with what you need to know about planting and living with them.

ASPARAGUS

Asparagus is a hardy, cool-season vegetable that, unlike most vegetable plants, comes back every year. Its tall vertical growth can be strikingly beautiful as well as delicious to eat. Although asparagus is moderately difficult to grow, the results are well worth it!

The asparagus plant reaches five to nine feet in height. It will spread from two to three feet wide and grows well in USDA hardiness zones two through eight.

The ideal germination temperature for seeds is between 70 and 77 degrees Fahrenheit. Asparagus prefers full sun exposure with a little shade. It is best to plant asparagus in acidic and dry soil that is well-drained and generously mixed with organic matter. The ideal soil pH is 7.0 but asparagus will tolerate wide variation.

Asparagus needs well-drained soil that is on the dry side and prefers morning sun with afternoon shade. It spreads, so plant this vegetable by itself at an edge of the garden, or in its own separate plot, so that it will not disturb the growth of other plants.

Plant asparagus crowns four to six weeks after the last frost. Dig an eight-inch-wide trench and set the roots into the trench, one to two inches deep before covering with a layer of soil. Place each crown three to four feet apart. As the shoots begin to emerge, cover them with additional soil until you've reached the surface level. Water asparagus well, but not too much. The crowns will rot with too much moisture. By the middle of summer, apply organic matter and mulch to help the soil retain moisture. Remove any weeds that sprout up through the feathery growth. Prevent beetle infestations by handpicking or spraying with a hard stream of water to knock them off. Should plants become infected with crown rot or wilt, remove the dead leaves. Do not include these leaves in your compost pile.

DANDELION

You may think this is an odd plant to put in the garden when you are usually trying to get rid of them in your yard. Dandelion leaves are often used in salads and even the flower, when it is yellow, is edible. They are full of vitamin A, B, C, D, iron, potassium and zinc. As you might imagine, dandelions are virtually indestructible. They grow in any type of soil, any climate, and are incredibly drought tolerant. Make sure to pick off the yellow flowers before they turn to seed or you will have more dandelions than you ever wanted, spreading out everywhere.

EGYPTIAN ONION

Egyptian onions are a rather strange vegetable, also known as walking onions. This plant is a self-propagating perennial that can serve as an interesting focal point in your yard. The vegetable is also delicious.

Egyptian onions are cool-season vegetables with a strong flavor similar to, but much more potent than, shallots. The plants are easy to cultivate and are very low maintenance. They are also called walking onions because they have the ability to relocate around your garden, replanting themselves. Consequently, you'll want to plant them in their own area, away from other vegetables. The plants grow to about two or three feet in height and spread up to two feet wide. They can easily survive frost and grow best in zones five to nine.

Egyptian onions prefer full sun exposure with a little shade. They grow best in well-drained soil mixed with organic matter and consistent moisture. You should aim for a soil pH of 6.2 to 6.8. Egyptian onions are grown from miniature bulblets. Plant them one-inch-deep into the soil and one foot apart, then just watch them go to town. After two years, divide the plants to give space for healthy further growth. The only pests that Egyptian onions are susceptible to are slugs, but these can be removed manually or by setting traps.

GARLIC

Garlic is not officially a perennial, but it is treated as such in temperate regions. Garlic is a cool season plant; it's an easily grown member of the onion family. Garlic produces white bulbs and is very frost-tolerant. In addition to its position as a staple ingredient in the kitchen, garlic is a natural insect repellent. The plant is also used in various healing remedies.

The plant grows between one and two feet tall and up to one foot wide. It requires full sun and well-drained, loamy soil mixed with lots of organic matter. Garlic tolerates many types of soil but it grows best in acidic soil with a pH of around 6.2 to 6.8.

If your region has harsh winters, you can plant garlic six to eight weeks before a hard frost. If you live in a warmer region, you can plant it sometime during February or March. Garlic grows well in raised beds. Do not plant it where you've grown onions or garlic in the past three years. I also recommend against planting store-bought garlic cloves, because they may be susceptible to disease. You can easily order garlic bulbs online or purchase them at a gardening center.

When it comes time to plant the bulbs, break them up, keeping the papery husks intact. Plant the cloves two inches deep and four to six inches apart, with their tips oriented upward. Rows should be planted one to two feet apart. Mulch garlic heavily after planting and remove the mulch around the sprouts, come spring. Garlic is generally not susceptible to pests, but it can become diseased, especially if over-soaked.

GLOBE ARTICHOKE

Globe artichokes are cool season vegetables and members of the thistle family. They blossom in mid-fall. The buds eventually grow into the artichokes we eat. When artichokes go unharvested, they transform into furry purple flowers that can beautify any garden.

Artichokes are a bit difficult to grow and may be best suited for an advanced gardener, but if planted properly the results can be astonishing. Globe artichokes can provide your garden with beautiful landscaping and delicious edibles for up to five years.

The plants grow up to six feet tall and spread out as far as four feet. In colder zones, it is suggested to plant them closer together to guard against early frost. They can tolerate frost but a heavy frost can damage their stalks. Globe artichokes grow best in warm zones but can survive mild winters with correct care. They grow between zones six and nine.

The ideal germination temperature for globe artichokes is 70 to 80 degrees, Fahrenheit. The plants require at least six hours of full sunlight. They require well-drained soil amended with plenty of compost at least to the depth of 2 feet. The soil can be sandy or loamy. Aim for a soil pH between 6.5 and 8.0.

Globe artichokes are heavy feeders. They require a moist environment, helped by generous mulching. They can survive dry conditions but may not produce as many flowering buds. As long as you use mulch to retain the moisture, you may get by with watering your globe artichokes less than once a week.

This plant requires plenty of space. Wait until a few weeks after the last frost before planting. Add five inches of compost to an eight-inch-deep trench. Dig the compost down about 12 inches into the garden. If you grow the plant from seeds, start them up to 12 weeks before the last frost; otherwise start by using basal stem pieces with the roots attached. Keep the plants well-mulched to hold in the moisture and feed them liquid fertilizer once a month during the growing season.

Watch for aphids, slugs and botrytis blight. Control aphids by washing off the plants with a stream of water every morning. For protection against slugs, use slug traps. If any part of the plant is damaged by botrytis blight, simply remove the diseased leaves and treat the healthier parts of the plant with fungicide.

JERUSALEM ARTICHOKE

Jerusalem artichokes, commonly referred to as sunchokes, are North American natives and part of the sunflower family. They grow underground using tubers that look like little potatoes. They can be grown almost anywhere in the US but the plant grows best in the north.

Between mid to late summer, Jerusalem artichokes produce yellow, daisy-like flowers on their stalks and sweet, edible tubers underground. It is a bit easier to grow Jerusalem artichokes than globe artichokes and they are quite a fascinating plant that can brighten up your garden and provide your household with an edible ingredient for your kitchen. However, they can become invasive if not carefully managed.

Jerusalem artichokes are tall plants, growing from six to 10 feet in height. Begin planting in early spring, using whole tubers or tuber pieces. To plant, set your starts in the row every two inches and cover them with three to five inches of soil Your rows should be at least three feet apart. Planting too late in the season can lower your yield.

Jerusalem artichokes love sandy soil that is well drained and full sun exposure. The soil should have an average pH of 7.0. You can place them so as to provide a little shade for shorter vegetables. Before planting, work a generous amount of compost into the soil. Once the plants begin to emerge and have grown at least 12 inches tall, mulch with organic matter to help retain soil moisture. Although the shade given off by the towering plant will reduce weed growth, it is still important to thoroughly weed anything that does crop up. Water your Jerusalem artichokes once a week. Gophers, slugs and snails can be a problem. Keep gophers and other small mammals out by building a fence. Chicken wire usually is sufficient. As for slugs and snails, monitor the plants for these pests and manually pick them off or set sticky traps to catch them when you're not around.

LOVAGE

The young leaves and stems from the lovage plant are delicious in salads and other dishes. It tastes remarkably like celery but without the crunch. The leaves grow up to six feet tall and are harvested in the spring while its leaves are still small and tender. The plant produces lovely clumps of flowers that attract beneficial insects to the garden.

Lovage is not picky about the soil it grows in, but it does need full sun to partial shade to thrive. The plant is hardy to zone four. Slugs and snails may pose a problem for lovage. Sprinkle a little sand beneath and around the plant to deter these pests.

RADICCHIO

Radicchio is a cool season chicory plant and a hardy biennial, which means it grows for two consecutive years. It has a sharp flavor and maroon leaves with flowers that form heads similar to cabbage. Radicchio is native to North Africa and Eurasia and can easily tolerate frost. It can be a difficult plant to grow, as it requires careful planning and timing, but if you can succeed, it will serve as a beautiful and edible plant for your garden.

Radicchio grows six inches to a foot tall and up to a foot in width. It grows best in zones four to eight. This plant requires full sun with a little shade and can adapt well to container gardens. It also requires well-drained and compost-laden soil. The germination temperature for radicchio is broad, ranging from 45 to 85 degrees Fahrenheit. Seedlings will emerge within seven to 10 days.

Start your seeds from four to six weeks indoors, but don't plant until after the last frost of the season. Space your seedlings four to five inches apart in rows that are two feet apart. Once seedlings emerge, thin them to 10 inches apart. After planting, use mulch to help preserve the soil moisture and weed thoroughly around the plants.

RAMPS

Ramps, also known as wild leeks, are of the onion family and have a very short growing period. They are thought of as a delicacy and some areas even celebrate the growing season with festivals. This vegetable grows only east of the Mississippi, usually in forests. It only appears in the spring and both the leaves and bulbs are edible. They have a garlicky smell with an onion flavor and are usually cooked by frying.

Ramps require shade and the moist, loamy soil that is found beneath the canopy of trees. They are hardy to zone four. The plant looks like green onions, with smooth flat light green leaves that are streaked with burgundy or purple.

RHUBARB

Rhubarb is a cool-season, hardy perennial that is tart in flavor and often used in jellies and desserts. Some people mistake rhubarb for a fruit, as it is often paired with other berries for cooking, but in reality, this plant is a vegetable. Rhubarb grows large, coarse, spiky green leaves (which are toxic, by the way) and produces white flowers. The edible part of this plant is the leaf stalk, which looks like celery but takes on a red or pink tinge. It has a tartness that requires lots of sugar or pairing with non-acidic fruits to tone down. It grows best in zones two to 9.

Rhubarb is easy to grow and simple to maintain. It emerges very early in the spring. Rhubarb's huge, roughly heart-shaped leaves grow on stalks that extend two to three feet in the air and can spread out to four or five feet wide. The plant blooms in early summer. It can tolerate frost although a bad frost in the spring can damage the leaves. Rhubarb requires six hours of sun and moist soil with excellent drainage. It is important to plant the crowns as soon as possible after spring arrives.

Plant rhubarb between one and three inches deep and two to three feet apart. You will want to place this plant where it can grow for years and not be disturbed. Mulch heavily to help preserve soil moisture and to kill invasive weeds. You do not need to fertilize rhubarb plants. Always cut off the flower stalks when they emerge to strengthen the growth of the plant. Wait for the second year for the plants to be established before you harvest the stems. Only water rhubarb when it gets very dry and water as closely to the roots as possible. If the plants get too crowded, divide the crowns and replant them further apart at least every five years.

Rhubarb is generally critter-resistant. However, it can be helpful to monitor the plants for potato stem borers, mites and curculio. Keep weeds to a minimum to prevent pests. Rhubarb can also be susceptible to fungal leaf spots and Phytophthora crown rot. To prevent these diseases, avoid crowding and overwatering. See that the plants receive good air circulation by keeping the weeds away and by ensuring adequate soil drainage.

For use in cooking, rhubarb freezes well, so feel free to clean and chop the stalks, then seal them up and place in the freezer until you have enough to use, or until you feel like baking a strawberry-rhubarb pie!

SALAD BURNET

Salad Burnet looks like a larger version of flat-leafed parsley. It has bright green leaves that taste like cucumber. Use it in green salads and pasta salads as an interesting flavor addition.

Salad burnet grows wild in dry, patchy soil. It is nearly indestructible, so it can be grown by almost anybody. This is one plant you'll want to start from seed, as it does not transplant well.

Space your seeds 12 inches apart, as the plant will reach up to 18 inches tall and grow up to 12 inches wide. It thrives in full sun or partial shade, in zones four to eight. Harvest the leaves frequently to keep the plant producing, cutting the stalks down to the base of the plant. If a flower forms, be careful to pinch it off before the blooms open. Leaf production will stop for the year if you let the plant bloom.

SCARLET RUNNER BEAN

Scarlet runner beans are usually grown as an ornamental plant, but the pods are edible, whether fresh or dried inside the pod. This plant will vine up to about nine feet tall, so it needs to be supported on a trellis. The leaves are green, but the pods range from light green to purple and must be picked young to eat fresh. The plant was named for its flowers, which bloom a brilliant red, making it a very attractive plant.

The scarlet runner bean is easily grown from seeds in a sunny area with well-composted soil. It doesn't need much encouragement to grow, but cold weather will kill it. It is best grown as a perennial in zones six and up. In the right conditions, this plant can produce annually for a long time; some plants have been known to live for over 20 years.

SORREL

Sorrel is a cool-season herb with a bitter, lemon-like flavor that is often used in soups, sauces and salads. The upper leaves of the plant turn a dark red and it buds into spiky, reddish green flowers.

There are three basic varieties of sorrel: **garden, French,** and **blood sorrel.** Garden sorrel is most common and will bloom early in the spring. French sorrel bears arrow-shaped leaves. Blood sorrel grows red leaves, prefers shade, and can only be harvested when young.

Sorrel grows up to two feet tall and six inches wide. It requires six hours of sunlight a day and needs well-drained soil. Sorrel tolerates frost, so you can begin working the soil two to three weeks before the last frost of the spring. Plant sorrel half an inch deep and two to three inches apart, separating the rows three to four feet apart.

It is important to water sorrel consistently. Aphids are the greatest danger, but they can easily be prevented by hosing down the plants periodically. Sorrel is highly resistant to disease.

SYLVETTA ARUGULA

Sylvetta Arugula is also called Wild Rocket; it comes from Italy. The plant has a spicy flavor that is a bit on the peppery side, but mixes well with other greens. The plant has pointed green leaves that are about six inches long. It prefers full sun, but will tolerate partial shade. This is a cool-temperature plant, but overly cold temperatures will kill it. The plant is a perennial in mild climates.

Add two inches of compost to the soil at least one to two weeks before the last anticipated frost of the year. Once the ground thaws, dig the compost in to at least a six-inch depth. Plant the seeds a quarter inch deep and about four to five inches apart. Keep the plant well watered and cut leaves as needed. Sylvetta Arugula grows best in cool climates, so gardeners who live in zone eight or warmer should plant in the fall while northern farmers will plant in early spring.

Chapter 2: Bloomin' Perennials

It is much less expensive, in the long run, to plant blooming perennials in your yard than annuals. Perennials may cost more initially, but they come back year after year with the right care.

When the temperature plummets, or the plants end their growing season, your annuals will die, leaving you to clean up the mess. Once you purchase a pot of daisies however, you will never need to re-purchase them, unless something goes drastically awry. In the winter, the plant will appear to die, but it is only dormant. Your daisies will sprout again next spring to bear flowers that are just as beautiful as the year before.

I'm not saying to never plant annuals; on the contrary, a mixture of perennials and annuals can make your yard a thing of beauty. Yet, at the moment we're focused on perennials, the anchor plants of your landscape. Once you have these long-lived flowers strategically placed, you can then install lively annuals that complement them in color, shape, texture, and size. The perennials will set your basic color palette, and then you can vary the overall color balance by using annuals to complete the display.

This chapter will describe some of the most useful perennials and will help you plant and maintain them. Don't worry, if you decide you don't like a flower in a specific spot, you can always start over next year. Start small, if you're unsure. Pick a few to plant in your yard and fill in around them with annuals for a profusion of summer color. If you like the mix, you can enlarge the look next year by adding more perennials for a profusion of blooms.

One thing you may notice when it comes to perennials. You will seldom be advised to start them from seed; it usually takes much too long and these plants are difficult to start. It may take several years before a perennial blooms. Some perennials are propagated by dividing an existing plant or by taking cuttings that will root in liquid over time. Some will grow from bulbs or rhizomes. Only occasionally will you be advised to plant perennials from seeds.

Here are some of the perennials that can enhance the attractiveness of your yard.

ASTERS

Asters resemble daisies, with their star-shaped flowers. They grow between eight inches and eight feet tall, depending on the variety. Many gardeners use asters as border plants; they also make a beautiful addition to rock gardens and wildflower areas, offering a blast of late summertime color, long after most other flowers have faded. Asters also attract butterflies, so you can enjoy moving color as they flutter around your yard.

The color of the blooms depends on the variety you have chosen. The King George variety yields large, dark blue flowers. The Silver Spray variety grows white flowers with a pink tinge. The Nanus aster displays star-shaped, light purple flowers.

Asters require three to six hours of sun daily. They grow best in zones three to eight in loamy, rich, well-drained soil. The best regions for growing asters have moist summers with cool night temperatures.

Plant your asters in early- to mid-spring. Seed germination can be inconsistent, so it is better to start them indoors during the winter. You start the plants by placing the seeds in the refrigerator for four to six weeks, then by planting them in seed trays and placing the trays in a sunny area to germinate.

When you're ready to plant your seeds in the ground, place them up to three feet apart, depending on how large your variety will grow. Water them immediately after planting and add a thick layer of mulch to help preserve soil moisture and minimize weed growth.

Add a small amount of compost to your flowers every spring. Water them regularly if you experience less than one inch of rain a week during the summer. Be careful not to over-water; too much moisture can cause asters to die. If your variety grows tall, use a stake or other type of support to keep them from falling over. After the foliage has died back in the fall, cut them back. Divide your asters every three years or so during the spring to help them maintain their vigor.

Asters are susceptible to aphids, mites, slugs, snails, and nematodes. They can also be affected by leaf spots, powdery mildew, and rust. You can guard against diseases by planting a disease-resistant variety.

ASTILBE

Astilbe is a perennial that displays beautiful, large feathery flowers in pink, red or white above large, fern-like leaves. They attract butterflies and the cut flowers add bright color to bouquets Unlike many plants, Astilbe plants prefer shade or partially shaded areas, making them great for adding some color to places where the sun doesn't reach. Never grow them in full sun, as the plant can sunburn. Astilbe grows best in zones three to nine. Some well-known varieties include Fanal, which produces crimson colored flowers, Irrlicht, with its white blooms, and Venus, which is known for its beautiful pink flowers. All three have rich, dark green leaves that provide a dramatic background for the blooms.

Astilbe plants grow best in well-drained, drier, loamy soil that has a slightly acidic to neutral pH. Their blooms are visible in spring and summer. Astilbe plants grow from six inches to five feet tall and from six inches to two feet wide, depending on the variety and the environmental conditions.

While it is possible to grow astilbe from seeds, germination is very difficult, so it is better to use plant divisions. Plant your starts in the spring or fall, spacing them one to three feet apart. If the divisions are bare-roots, plant them in a hole that is twice the width of the plant, four to six inches deep. Spread out the roots and position them pointing downward into the soil. Leave the crown of the plant two inches below the ground. Once the roots are in place, cover them with soil and pack it firmly.

Astilbe plants should remain moist. If your region does not experience adequate rainfall, water their roots deeply. Apply an organic fertilizer every season to ensure vigorous blooming. When Astilbe plants begin to multiply, they develop clumps. Every four years you'll want to divide your clumps as soon as the crown grows above ground in the spring. Anything you choose not to replant elsewhere would make a welcome gift to other gardeners.

After your astilbe plants have bloomed, cut off the flower stems. This will not help the plant produce more flowers, but will improve their appearance. Astilbes are most susceptible to the tarnished leaf bug, powdery mildew, and bacterial leaf spots.

BERGENIAS

Bergenias, also known as elephant's ears, are perennial, partial-evergreen plants with coarse, leather-like ragged-edged leaves and flowers that bloom in white, pink, deep red or dark purple. In colder regions, the leaves will become red or bronze-colored in autumn. Bergenias originated in Central Asia, but are a popular perennial in many home gardens. The bergenia's blooms only last for a couple of weeks, but the flowers are gorgeous. Even without its blooms, the bergenia's unique leaves are eye-catching in any garden.

Bergenias grow between one and two feet tall and up to two feet wide. They thrive best in zones four through 10. Plant them in the autumn or in early spring. Bergenias grow best in partial sun and rich soil, but are tolerant of shade and can live in full sun or less than ideal soil. It is important to water bergenias regularly to sustain their growth.

BLACK-EYED SUSAN

Black-eyed Susans, or Rudbeckia, are perennials that grow wild across North America. They bloom between the summer and fall, delighting viewers with their bright yellow and sometimes orange to red flower petals. Their name originates from the prominent black center of their flower. Black-eyed Susans often grow in groups. Insects that are attracted to their nectar boost their pollination.

Black-eyed Susans grow to at least three feet in height, if not taller. Their blooms are often up to three inches wide. Since these flowers easily spread through pollination and can be pretty invasive, it is probably best to grow them away from other plants.

Black-eyed Susans grow best in zones three to nine. They require at least six hours of sun per day. In the United States, it is best to start planting them between March and May. The soil temperature should be at least 70 degrees, Fahrenheit. Germination can take anywhere from one week to a month and is inconsistent, so it is better to use divisions or transplants, setting them in the soil in late May.

This flower prefers damp soil with excellent drainage. As far as watering goes, water based on the dryness of your soil. Checking regularly for dryness can help you determine when and how much you should water. Deadhead the spent flowers and divide the plants every few years to help promote healthy growth.

Black-eyed Susans are most susceptible to fungal diseases caused by overcrowding, as well as aphids, slugs, snails, leaf spots, rust, and powdery mildew. They are deer-resistant and attract butterflies to your garden. Black-eyed Susans will re-seed after their first blooming. The best varieties are Becky Mixed, Sonora, and Toto.

BLANKET FLOWER/GALLARDIA

The blanket flower starts blooming in one color and progresses to others seamlessly. Its bloom is daisy-like with a central dark brown-to-red disc and petals like a daisy. The petals may start out burgundy-colored, but will change to orange and then to bright yellow, causing them to look very much like an American Indian blanket, hence the name. The "Arizona" variety only grows to about 10 inches tall, but it produces orange-, red-, and yellow-tipped flowers. The "Burgundy" blanket flower produces three-inch-wide wine-red flowers on 24- to 30-inch-tall stems.

The blanket flower grows from 18 to 24 inches tall and the leaves are toothed and greenish-silver, with a hairy appearance. It grows best in zones three through nine and blooms from summer into fall, attracting bees and butterflies.

Plant your blanket flower starts in late spring or early fall. Space them 12 inches apart in full sun. The blanket flower will tolerate just about any type of soil. Deadhead the flower heads to encourage additional blooming. The blanket flower does multiply, so you'll want to divide the plants every two to three years.

MARIGOLD

The marigold, also known as calendula, is a ferny-leafed plant that produces deep orange to bright yellow blooms. This plant has been used as medicine for centuries, but its beauty qualifies it to grow in any flower garden.

The marigold tolerates any type of soil, even the poorest, and prefers full sun but will grow in partial shade. The plant has branching stems and grows about 12 inches tall. You'll want to plant them two to three feet apart. I've started marigolds by seed outdoors and I've also successfully started them indoors, about six weeks before the last frost, then transplanted them outside.

You'll want to remove spent flowers to keep the plants blooming all summer long. Marigold flowers are edible, with a slightly bitter taste.

The plant is considered a short-lived perennial. It will survive the winter in mild climates, but cold climates will kill it off. The plant does tend to reseed if spent flowers are left on the plants and allowed to fall to the ground.

CLEMATIS

Clematis is a vining plant that produces a breathtaking array of star-shaped flowers with fuzzy, star-like centers. They bloom in a variety of colors, with some varieties producing multi-colored flowers. The vines are woody and can grow beyond 20 feet long. They require a trellis or other form of climbing support. Some varieties produce flowers five to six inches apart, while others bloom more densely. The most popular varieties produce red to white, lavender to deep purple, or yellow blossoms. Blooms vary from single to double and some are bell-shaped.

Clematis plants enjoy full sun and well-drained soil. A single plant is capable of filling a trellis. Cover the roots with mulch to keep them cool and moist during hot months and warm during cold months. Cut the vine back nearly to the ground after the first frost has killed it back.

CHRYSANTHEMUM

Chrysanthemums are one of the few fall-flowering perennials. They bloom in a plethora of colors, shapes, and sizes. Always be sure you purchase a perennial chrysanthemum that will come back next year; many of the plants sold during the fall are annuals that will not come back. Chrysanthemum blooms may be shaped like a cushion, a spider, a pompom, or a daisy, depending on the variety. They bloom in red, orange, bronze, purple, white, or yellow.

Single-petaled varieties can look much like daisies, with hairy stems and toothed leaves. The plants grow shorter than most daisies at about 12 inches high. The plant and blooms grow in a tight-packed mound. The cushion variety forms flowers that are medium-sized and actually look like a cushion or a flattened haystack.

More decorative varieties have large elaborate blossoms with many rows of petals that curl toward the center. Anemone-type blooms are shaped like a plump round cushion with a center of shorter, darker colored petals. Pompom type chrysanthemums produce small firm globes with light-colored petals. The quill variety has tubular petals that curve at their ends; Spider chrysanthemums produce flowers made of long tubular petals curved at their ends to resemble spider legs. Spoon varieties have flat petals that curl at their tips into a shape that looks like the bowl of a spoon.

Chrysanthemums prefer early sun and about five to six hours of it per day. They prefer loamy, well-drained soil. Plant from containers early spring after the first frost or six weeks before the first frost of the season. Space plants 18 to 24 inches apart. If you plant in the spring, pinch off the flowers continually until late August to encourage a fall blooming.

CONEFLOWER/ECHINACEA

Coneflowers are brightly colored perennials that resemble daisies and have raised centers. They are sometimes used as herbal medicines. Their flowers are pink, red, white, or purple. The seeds contained in the flower heads are attractive to songbirds.

Coneflowers are popular garden additions because they are easy to maintain, they can survive in dry conditions better than most other plants, and they make beautiful bouquets. They bloom in the summer and fall and grow best in zones three to nine.

It is possible to plant coneflower from seeds, but they most likely will not bloom the first year. Start by loosening the soil in your planting site to at least a foot deep and mix in four inches of compost. Coneflowers grow best in soil that is well-drained, humus-rich, and loamy. If you are transplanting them from a pot, place them in a hole that is twice their size, making sure that the root is level with the soil. The ideal time to plant coneflowers is in March or April. They thrive in full sun but will still bloom in partial shade. Plant coneflowers one to three feet apart and water deeply after planting.

Every spring, put a small layer of compost around your coneflowers, followed by a thick layer of mulch to help retain soil moisture and keep away the weeds. If your region experiences less than one inch of rain per week, water coneflowers on a regular basis. If your coneflowers become floppy and unstable, tie them to a stake to keep them upright and cut them down to the ground after they bloom. You can often prolong their productive season by cutting off dead flowers.

Coneflowers are most susceptible to leaf miners, powdery mildew, gray mold, bacterial spots, and vine weevils.

CORAL BELLS/ALUMROOT

Coral bells, also known as alumroot, are hardy perennials with intense, frilly, green or bronze leaves and brightly colored flowers that bloom in spring and summer. The bell-like flowers can range in color from white to bright red and are a hummingbird magnet. The leaves grow six to eight inches long and the flower stalks can grow up to three feet tall.

The plants make great ground cover and can serve well as supplemental edging. Coral bells don't grow very well from seed, so it is usually best to purchase starts. They are limited to zones three through nine

Since coral bells appear naturally in forests, they prefer shade and need rich soil with excellent drainage. Plant coral bells in the fall or the spring. Place the root ball at the same level as the surface of the soil. Deadhead spent blooms to encourage long-lasting flowers and cut back the plant in the spring. You can apply a small amount of mulch and compost around your plants to help preserve soil moisture. If your area is particularly dry, you will want to water coral bells regularly. Divide these plants every few years. They are susceptible to weevils, powdery mildew, bacteria and botrytis.

COREOPSIS

Coreopsis is a perennial wildflower that grows stalks with wispy leaves, topped off by brightly colored orange or yellow flowers. Coreopsis blooms are hardy and long-lived; they can easily withstand dry conditions. The plant appears naturally in the Southeastern United States; it is fairly easy to maintain. The coreopsis plant will bloom from June to October and thrives in zones three to nine.

The Moonbeam coreopsis is a variety that displays yellow flowers on foot-high plants. However, this variety is not as hardy as most others. The Grandiflora coreopsis grows two feet tall and bears golden blooms. The Zagreb coreopsis is a drought-hardy variety that grows between 12 and 18 inches tall and produces dark orange blossoms.

The coreopsis plant prefers at least six hours of sun daily. It grows to between one and three feet tall and slowly spreads to a maximum of 18 inches wide. The plant prefers dry, well-drained soil. You can propagate coreopsis by seed, from cuttings, or by division.

Coreopsis plants do not require a great deal of attention. Take cuttings in the spring and deadhead the blooms to encourage additional flower production. Cut the plant back at the end of summer to encourage fall blooming, then cut it back again in the spring. Divide the plants every few years to help them maintain their vigor.

Coreopsis plants are most susceptible to aphids, slugs, snails, striped beetles, and flea beetles. Watch out for powdery mildew, downy mildew, root rot, crown rot, leaf spots, and blight. This plant can help keep deer away from your property, while attracting butterflies and beneficial insects to your garden.

DAISY

The simple daisy is probably the most recognizable perennial of them all, with a central golden disc surrounded by rays of white petals. The flowers grow on long stems with an abundance of green feathery leaves. Most daisy varieties grow anywhere from 24 to 32 inches tall. The most popular variety, the Shasta daisy, grows about three feet tall and the plant may spread out as wide as two feet.

This is a great container plant to set out in late spring. It requires well-drained soil and full sun to flourish, but will tolerate poor soil and partial shade. It thrives in zones three through nine. Daisies do not bloom until the second year but they bloom all summer long. Slugs, snails, and aphids can become a problem. Divide your daisies every three to four years to encourage prolific blooming.

DIANTHUS/PINKS

Dianthus, or pinks as they are also known, are part of the carnation family; they produce beautiful pink, red, and white flowers that are best recognized by their light spicy, cinnamon-like smell. Many people use Dianthus as garden borders or as potted plants. They grow between six inches and three feet tall. Their flowers have a central disk surrounded by ragged petals. The blooms are primarily pink, although they can vary from shades of red to white. Their leaves are thin and dispersed but their stems are quite substantial. Dianthus plants prefer full sun to slight shade and soil that is fertile, well-drained, and neutral pH.

Plant dianthus after the last frost, leaving two to three feet between each plant. Dianthus require watering when dry but avoid getting their leaves wet. Apply a general fertilizer every six to eight weeks and deadhead the flowers for better blooming. After your dianthus stops blooming in the fall, cut the stalks back to the ground. When your plants sprout in the spring, remove any dead leaves that remain from the previous year.

FORGET-ME-NOT

The precious blue flowers of low-growing forget-me-nots are one of the first flowers to welcome the spring. The plant grows from six to 12 inches tall with fuzzy green stems, lacy leaves, and tiny quarter-inch blue or pink flowers with yellow centers. Forget-me-nots love moisture and grow well near streams or ponds, but they can also flourish in gardens, just as long as they get enough moisture. They tolerate poor soil but must be planted in an area where there is partial to full shade.

There is a biennial forget-me-not that only blooms in the spring, but your perennial version will bloom as long as it is shaded and the roots stay cool, usually via mulching. Plant clumps of forget-me-nots in the spring, as soon as the earth can be worked. Space the plants about a foot apart. If you live in a moderate climate, you can start seeds directly in the soil in the fall and they will sprout the following spring.

FOXGLOVE

Foxgloves are flowering biennials that grow as perennials in warm climates. Even in colder climates, they tend to reseed, providing a steady supply in your garden. The foxglove produces groups of tubular-shaped flowers that grow on stalks extending up to six feet in height. The flowers are white, pink, yellow, purple, or red and are often spotted. Foxglove plants grow vertically and may require staking or another type of support system. They grow best in zones four through 10.

The hotter the climate, the more shade your foxgloves will require. It is best to plant them in at least partial shade. The foxglove thrives in well-drained, moist, and rich soil. You'll want to keep the soil damp but not overly wet.

If you grow foxgloves from seed, it will take them two years to bloom. If you do not want them to re-seed, you will need to deadhead the flowers; otherwise, just let them grow, giving you a steady presence of foxgloves. The blooms look beautiful in bouquets and are equally impressive in your garden. Since the flowers are poisonous, you'll want to keep them away from small children and pets. However, they're not poisonous to hummingbirds, which love foxglove nectar.

HARDY HIBISCUS

Hibiscus are colorful, bushy summer plants that attract butterflies and songbirds to your garden. They produce white to red flowers. The hardy variety is a perennial that thrives up to zone five and produces colorful round flowers amid heart-shaped foliage. The flowers are large, up to a foot in diameter and the plant can reach up to seven feet tall.

Plant your hibiscus in early fall or late spring. Prepare the soil by working it down six inches and adding in compost and organic matter. The planting hole should be as deep as the original container and you should space each plant four to five feet apart.

Hibiscus plants require full sun and well-drained soil that is rich and moist. These plants naturally grow near wet areas such as swamps, so it is important to keep them watered regularly in the summer. In the winter, mulch them to keep the water away; otherwise their roots could sustain damage. Blooms should appear in late summer. Although the blossoms don't last very long, you can count on the plant growing back every year. Since the hardy hibiscus is a heavy feeder, you'll want to apply an organic fertilizer with a high phosphorous content. In the fall, cut back any dead portions of the plant.

HELLEBORE/LENTEN OR CHRISTMAS ROSE

Hellebores are perennials with a unique winter blooming season. Many species of Hellebore are evergreen and herbaceous; they bloom in winter or very early spring. This plant is hardy to zone four. It also tolerates shade well. Hellebore has leather-like, concave foliage with drooping groups of light green flowers that have a dark red edging. The blooms are long-lived and emit a pleasant fragrance. Hellebores are very easy to maintain once they are established. Just be careful to keep them out of the reach of children and pets, because the flower can be deadly if eaten.

You can grow hellebores from seeds or divisions. They prefer well-drained organic soil with filtered sunlight. For best results, choose an area that is naturally shaded. Plant hellebores in the fall; they require two months of a moist chilling before they will bloom. The only difficulty of starting hellebores from seeds is that they can take up to four years to bloom.

Keep the soil wet to help promote plant growth. Regularly discard any leaves that appear damaged. Fertilize hellebores in the fall and again in the spring with bone meal.

The most popular species of hellebore are Helleborus *orientalis*, Helleborus *foetidus* and Helleborus *niger*. *Orientalis* is the earliest winter bloomer and comes in a vast array of colors. *Foetidus* produces textured green flowers that may include dark red edging; the name comes from its unpleasant (fetid) odor. *Niger* produces pure white blooms that can grow three inches high.

HONEYSUCKLE

Honeysuckle is a perennial vine well-known for its pleasant smell and sweet nectar. The honeysuckle makes a bright addition to any garden with its red and yellow blooms that are highly resistant to heat and easy to maintain. These plants grow almost anywhere in the United States and sometimes grow as year-round, depending on the region.

Honeysuckle vines prefer full sun but a little shade won't harm them. The vine thrives in almost any type of soil, if it is well-drained and mixed with organic matter. You may find it helpful to plant honeysuckle with a trellis if you don't want it to grow low to the ground. Plant seeds or divisions after the last frost of the spring, spacing them three feet apart.

Water your honeysuckle regularly. Prune frequently if you're growing them low to the ground, to prevent them from taking over your entire garden. Pruning is best done in the fall or winter, while the plant is dormant. Apply mulch to prevent weeds and to help protect the roots during cold weather.

HOSTA

Hostas are well-known perennials that are most commonly used in shady areas. Their wide green, blue or variegated cream and green leaves grow together in clumps. Lovely trumpet-like white or purple flowers appear on stems in the middle of the summer; these flowers attract bees and hummingbirds to the garden. Hostas prefer partial sun to full shade; too much sun can burn the leaves.

When choosing the location for hostas, you'll want to allow enough room for them to develop. Plants should be spaced at least 10 inches apart. The plants thrive in rich, well-drained soil with a slightly elevated pH. They require regular watering and frequent application of a balanced fertilizer to help stimulate their growth. Although hostas can be pretty rugged, they are still susceptible to snails, slugs, and deer. To prevent snails and slugs from troubling your plants, spread sand around each base.

LARKSPUR / DELPHINIUM

Larkspurs, also known as delphiniums, are beautiful perennial plants that bloom in bold shades of purple, blue, pink and white. Despite their beauty and popularity, they can be a bit trickier to plant and maintain than most perennial flowers but the work is definitely worthwhile. The larkspur requires a support system to hold it upright and needs a geography region that experiences cool and damp summers. It grows best in zones three to seven. Larkspur is easily damaged by wind and rain so you will also need to take that into consideration when designing your garden.

The larkspur plant requires full to partial sunlight and grows best in well-drained, loamy, and alkaline soil. Start working the soil in the spring by adding in a thick layer of compost. It is challenging to grow larkspur from seed, I recommend using starts. During the spring, add in a mixture of wood ashes and lime to boost the soil's alkaline levels.

Add in a support system when the plants have reached one foot tall. A garden stake will do the trick. If you experience inadequate rainfall in your area, water your larkspur regularly. This plant is very thirsty during its growth period and requires a dose of balanced fertilizer every couple of weeks. You'll want to deadhead the flowers as they die. Larkspur attracts butterflies but is susceptible to cyclamen mites, snails, and slugs. It is also known to fall prey to powdery mildew, fungal spots, crown rot, root rot, Southern blight, and smut.

LEWISIA

Lewisia is a perennial with dark green foliage with brightly colored flowers. The plant was named after Meriwether Lewis, who discovered it in the mountainous areas of Western North America in the early 1800s. Native Americans have used the root for centuries to treat sore throats.

Lewisia is a simple yet hardy plant that thrives in zones three to eight. The foliage grows low to the ground, rarely reaching more than three inches in height. The stems and blooms themselves can grow up to one foot tall.

The easiest way to plant lewisia is through transplants or container plants. You can start it from seed but it will take a few seasons to become established. Lewisia grows best in sandy soil that is well drained. It needs to be fertilized monthly with a granulated fertilizer. The plant also requires a consistent amount of water, but overwatering can lead to root rot if drainage is insufficient. Lewisia is most susceptible to slugs and snails, but other pests should not be a problem. .

NICOTIANA

Nicotiana is a perennial member of the tobacco family that flowers with a perfume-like fragrance. It is native to the warmer regions of North and South America. Nicotiana is easy to grow and blooms during afternoons beginning in early summer and continuing throughout the growing season. The flowers can range from hues of red and yellow to white and lavender. Depending on their variety, nicotiana plants grow between one and three feet tall. It is best to grow them in groups to get the most out of their pleasant smell.

Nicotiana plants require full sun with a little shade and need rich, well-drained soil. It is also helpful to add compost into the soil before you plant them. Apply a fertilizer with a high level of phosphorous upon planting and then once a month afterward. Nicotiana likes plenty of water and moist soil.

You can propagate the nicotiana directly from seeds or you can start them indoors. The earlier you start them indoors, the sooner you will see their blooms. Plant outdoors as soon as the last frost has passed. Seeds should be covered with an eighth inch of starting soil. It will take about two to three weeks for the seeds to germinate.

The leaves of nicotiana plants are sticky; they easily catch debris and other foreign objects, so it is important to apply compost and fertilizer with caution. Anything that sticks to the leaves may damage them. After the plants bloom, prune and deadhead them to your liking.

Some important things to know about nicotiana plants are that they will drop seeds throughout the growing season. These seeds are poisonous if ingested by children or pets. The plant is susceptible to fungal diseases, aphids, and gnats. Otherwise, nicotiana is generally easy to maintain and has the advantage of attracting hummingbirds.

PHLOX

Phlox is a wild perennial that has basically two formats. The creeping varieties grow low to the ground and are used as ground cover. Tall garden phlox lives up to its name, producing the same brilliant flowers, but on a much longer stem.

Creeping phlox blooms only in the spring and creates a carpet of vivid color. Its small leaves remain green throughout the growing season. Tiny star-shaped flowers cover the entire plant. Phlox bloom in red, lavender, pink, white, and bluish-purple. Plants only grow to four or six inches tall but spread out for about two feet. The creeping phlox requires full sun to partial shade and moist, well-drained soil. When you plant creeping phlox, set them in at soil level, making sure none of the stems are buried. Cut them back after the first flowering in the spring and you just may get another blooming cycle. Pruning also encourages stem growth. Divide creeping phlox every two to three years.

Tall garden phlox blooms all summer, producing large clusters of pink, purple, lavender, or white flowers. It works well in back borders since it grows three to four feet high. It requires partial to full sun and grows best in zones two through nine. The easiest way to start tall garden phlox is from transplants rather than from seeds. Space the plants 18 to 24 inches apart to give them room to grow and water them immediately after placing in the ground. Divide tall garden phlox every two years.

PINCUSHION FLOWER

Pincushion flowers are easy to grow and maintain. The plants bear ruffled flowers on fragile stems. They often attract butterflies and can last all season if planted and cared for correctly. The typical bloom time for the pincushion flower is spring to winter. Pincushion flowers are hardy and grow best in zones five to nine. The average plant can grow up to a foot tall and one foot wide.

Pincushion flowers prefer full sunlight with a little shade. They will thrive in well-drained soil. Even if they do grow in clay soil, they will not bloom again and will live only for a season or two. Water pincushion flowers while their roots are growing. Once their roots are established, they can easily withstand droughts and dry conditions. It is helpful to deadhead them and apply a little balanced fertilizer to encourage healthy blooms.

The best varieties of pincushion flowers are "Black Knight," "Butterfly Blue," and "Pink Mist."

POPPY

Poppies grow as annuals or perennials, depending on the variety. Iceland poppies, Oriental poppies and Alpine poppies are all perennial varieties. The seeds have been used for centuries in foods and for healing purposes.

Poppies are best known for their colorful blooms. Oriental poppies grow well in zones four to nine while Alpine poppies grow better in zones five to eight.

The plant can grow as tall as 48 inches, with flower petals up to six inches in length. Poppies require full sun and thrive in well-drained soil. Add a thick layer of compost to the top six inches of soil during the fall. Plant poppy seeds on top of the soil, spacing them three inches apart and covering them lightly with soil. Throughout the fall and winter, lightly water the soil whenever it looks dry. It will take about two weeks for poppy seeds to germinate. When the seedlings are about two inches tall, thin them to six inches apart.

Once the poppies reach full maturity, you'll only need to water them once a week with one inch of water. You can apply a thick layer of mulch around the plants to help retain moisture and to prevent weeds from growing. Regular deadheading during the season is encouraged. During the first spring and the middle of the first year's summer, apply a balanced fertilizer to your poppies.

ROSE

Roses are really a shrub, but over the years, the attention has shifted from the plant to its blooms. There are thousands of rose varieties, ranging from miniatures to climbing roses, and they come in all sorts of colors. The most popular type is the tea rose, with its long stems. The blooms do not have much of a fragrance, but they are very beautiful. These are part of the hybrid class of roses.

Old roses do have fragrance but do not have that perfect appearance we usually require in bouquets. Singles have lobed petals extending daisy-like from a center. Complex roses have multiple layers of petals that build up into a full bloom. The cabbage rose has so many layers of petals that it mounds up and looks almost like, well, a cabbage. There are an abundance of rose varieties; Gallicas, Grandiflora, Centifolis, and Floribunda, are just a few of the most popular .

All roses prefer full sun and soil that has been amended with a great deal of compost. They bloom from late spring into the fall. To avoid diseases, do not crowd rose plants. Because of their thorns — which you can't have a rose without — always wear protective gloves when working with them. Deadhead any spent flowers to encourage additional blooming.

Roses require lots of water, but keep the water down at the base of the plant. Too much water on the leaves just begs for disease to set in. Never give roses just a little water; they need to be watered deeply. A soaker hose is highly recommended in climates where rain does not provide enough moisture. Use two to three inches of mulch to help preserve the moisture.

Roses require regular pruning, but never cut them back after the leaves start to emerge in the spring. In early spring, prune out any old stalks that are thicker than a number two pencil. Prune to keep the plant open and airy. After October first, stop pruning in cold climates.

Roses do have problems with aphids and are susceptible to many diseases, although the newer varieties are somewhat disease resistant. Common diseases include blackspot, powdery mildew, botrytis and mosaic.

RUSSIAN SAGE

Russian sage is a woody, shrub that is easy to plant and simple to maintain. It has silvery white stems with feathery leaves that produce lavender-colored flowers on their tips. Certain varieties will weep as they mature while others will grow upright. This plant grows best in zones five to nine. Russian sage grows between three and five feet tall and up to three feet wide. It prefers full sun and is tolerant of dry conditions. Russian sage is a late bloomer; flowers will not begin to appear until late summer.

It is possible to grow Russian sage from seed but the germination process will take some time, generally up to four months. Seeds need to be kept moist and warm during the germination process. It may take a few years for them to bloom after germination.

An easier way to add Russian sage to your property is to purchase container plants. Unlike many plants, the Russian sage can be planted anytime during the growing season. Space the plants two to three feet apart to provide ample room for growth and water well after transplanting into your garden.

Russian sage plants are not picky about their soil and will grow in almost any climate, withstanding drought conditions. Once the plants are settled, cut them back by half a foot each spring. In warm climates, deadhead the flowers to promote a strong, second bloom. Established plants can spread fairly quickly, so remove unwanted startups, complete with their roots, to prevent spreading. Divide Russian sage every four to six years to sustain healthy, productive plants. Division will also slow their tendency to spread.

SALVIA

Salvia is an herbaceous perennial with bush-like foliage and spikes of blooms. Salvia plants typically grow between one and five feet tall, although most varieties hover around three feet in height. Their flowers are typically bright or dark red in color, but they can also bloom in other colors. Salvia is easy to grow and care for once established. It is not generally susceptible to pests or diseases.

Salvia requires full sun and thrives in average, well-drained soil. It is important to think wisely about placement, because this plant will aggressively re-seed. Apply a general fertilizer at the time of planting and then once per month. Water once a week during dry conditions. It is important to weed thoroughly around the plants...or you can apply some mulch and let it do most of the weeding for you!

SEDUM

Sedum is a perennial that boasts thick, oval leaves, thick stems, and small clusters of flowers. There are several varieties of sedum that can serve different purposes to your garden. Stonecrop varieties grow low to the ground and are used as ground cover or to grace rock gardens. Tall varieties are used as borders and make a great addition to any bouquet.

Sedums are a wonderful plant if you are a beginning gardener. They grow in zones three through nine and bloom in a range of warm colors. The foliage itself could display as blue, green, chartreuse, gray, silver, purple or burgundy. Most sedums look like succulents. Autumn Joy and Purple Emperor are popular tall sedums while Jenny's Stonecrop is a great yellow sedum.

Sedum plants require full sun with well-drained loamy or sandy soil. It is best to space each tall plant half a foot apart and plant stonecrop varieties three feet apart. Container plants are the best way to add Sedum to your landscape. Once they are planted, most of the hard work is done. You should monitor the plants and water them when they appear dry.

Sedums are most susceptible to slugs, snails, mealybugs, and scaled insects. However, they can also be inviting to butterflies. The most popular varieties of sedum are the Sedum Humifusum and Brilliant. Sedum Humifusum is a ground-covering variety with yellow flowers. The Brilliant sedum will produce bright pink flowers.

VERONICA

Veronica is an easy-to-maintain perennial that boasts long spiky blue, white, purple, and pink flowers that can grow between one and three feet tall. Veronica also appears in a bush variety that can grow quite wide and up to 10 feet tall. One variety, Crater Lake Blue, is a ground-covering variety that can grow up to nearly two feet tall and will bloom around June. The Red Fox variety will produce pink, ground-hugging flowers.

Veronica requires at least six hours of sun and thrives in fertile, loamy and well-drained soil. It is best to grow veronica in zones three to 11. For the best results, transplant in the spring. Use veronica from container plants for best results. Water well when you first transplant them into your garden and then water consistently if you experience little rain during the summer.

The non-bush variety requires the addition of a stake or other type of support system to allow it to grow vertically. Surround your plants with a layer of mulch throughout the growing season and add a thick layer of mulch to retain soil moisture. To propagate veronica, divide it every couple years in either the fall or the spring.

Veronica is susceptible to scale insects and a few diseases including downy mildew, powdery mildew and root rot. However, they are wonderful for attracting birds and butterflies.

The flowering plants I've mentioned in this chapter are just a small sampling of all the perennials you can use to add color and variety to your landscape. As your plants thrive year after year, you will have ample starts to give to friends and neighbors. Most of these flowers are generated from container plants or transplants, so they may cost a pretty penny to get started. But considering their longevity and low-maintenance character, you will find them a worthwhile investment.

Chapter 3: Grasses, Shrubs, And Foliage Plants

Many grasses, foliage plants, and shrubs are suitable for the landscape in your home garden. Grasses grow tall and graceful, providing great backgrounds for smaller plants. You can also use them to screen unsightly utility boxes. Foliage plants also serve well as background plants, but they can also be used as ground cover. Most perennial shrubs bloom, making them a colorful addition as a foundation plant or as a spectacular focal point in your garden.

PERENNIAL ORNAMENTAL GRASSES

BLUE FESCUE

Blue fescue forms short small mounds of blue grass. There are several varieties of fescue but most grow a foot tall and about one foot wide. They have slender blades that resemble a porcupine. Fescue does well in zones four to eight and is tolerant of all climates except for extreme heat. It thrives in almost any type of soil. Flowers will appear on long stems in June. Most people like the blooms, but if you don't, it is perfectly fine to cut the flower stalks to maintain the mounding shape.

This is the perfect no-fuss plant. It prefers full sun to partial shade and well-drained soil. It is an evergreen in mild climates; in more severe winters, the blades will die back and turn brown. The only maintenance needed for blue fescue is to run your fingers through the mounds periodically to remove any of the brown blades. Blue fescue does not do well in extreme heat, but regular summer heat in the 80s and even 90s does not seem to bother it.

Plant your fescue starts about a foot apart, after the last frost of spring or in late summer to early fall. If you plant in the fall, ensure that you have four to five weeks of warm weather left.

Fescue does not require any fertilization, but it will be very happy if you apply a few inches of compost every spring.

FEATHER REED GRASS

Feather reed grass also clumps, but it grows taller than fescue. It will reach up to six feet tall and six feet wide and does best in zones five to nine. This grass prefers full sun and well-drained soil. The blades are green, but the feathery flowers that grow on stalks are bluish-purple or pink. The seeds are sterile, so the plant will not propagate.

Set transplants far apart as they grow to about six feet across. Actually, one plant may be all you need, unless you have a massive yard. Cut the plant back to three inches above the ground in the winter, or in the spring before it starts to sprout again. Divide your feather reed plant every three to four years, so the center of the plant does not die out.

FOUNTAIN GRASS

Fountain grass is so-named because the blades look much like a water fountain reaching to the sky and then cascading back down. This grass also has a mounding habit with green blades. The flowers are silvery, feather-like plumes that shimmer in the sunlight. The plant grows best when planted in full sun in well-drained soil in zones five to nine. Fountain grass is highly drought tolerant.

Set your transplants in the spring or summer, giving them plenty of room to grow. Fountain grass can expand beyond six feet, both tall and wide. Cut this grass back to three inches from the ground in winter or early spring.

LITTLE BLUESTEM

Little bluestem grass is very tough and grows just about anywhere in any condition. It has gray-green blades that turn purple, red, or orange in autumn. It does prefer full sun and well-drained soil, but will grow in the worst soil you can imagine.

It grows about three feet tall and can be invasive. Little bluestem flowers grow on stems and produce fluffy seed balls. The wind blows them just like dandelions and – like dandelions – they easily take root in the soil and start growing. If you don't want little bluestem plants cropping up everywhere, I suggest you cut off the flowers before they mature into seeds.

You can grow little bluestem from seed or by transplanting. In either case, set the plants about four feet apart to give them room to spread. This grass does not need any encouragement to grow. Apply compost around the roots in the spring but do not use fertilizer. Little bluestem is often used for erosion control and it will go dormant in a drought, but will come back strong when the drought ends.

MAIDENGRASS

Maidengrass has narrow, arching blades that are solid green or variegated. It produces beautiful silver plumes late in the summer. The plant grows to eight feet tall and about 10 feet wide with a clumping habit. It does best in zones five through nine. The foliage changes to bronze and burgundy in the fall.

Transplant maidengrass in the soil at the same level it was in the pot. Sometimes the center of the plant will dry out and die. If that happens, divide the roots and replant. Cut maidengrass back to three inches from the ground in the winter or early spring and divide the plant every three years.

PAMPAS GRASS

Pampas grass grows fast and large in clumps of lush green grass with creamy white plumes for flowers. The plant grows five to 10 feet tall and may spread more than five feet. This plant can be invasive.

Set transplants in areas of full sun to partial shade and in moist, well-drained soil. This plant is tolerant of wind, drought and salt spray, which is why you may see pampas grass growing on beaches. It grows in zones seven to eleven and should be placed in a protected area in cold regions.

Prune the plant to the ground in late winter or early spring and it will come back year after year.

SEA OATS

Sea oats is a grass that grows two to three feet tall and is comfortable in zones five to nine. It sprouts green blades in the summer that turn to copper or bronze in the fall. The blades are reminiscent of bamboo. The seeds begin to appear in late summer and look like oats hanging from a slender stem. The appearance of sea oats is light and airy lending a refreshing look to dried flower arrangements.

Sea oats is drought tolerant. Transplant starts in areas of full sun to partial shade. Give your sea oats plenty of room to multiply; you may have only one plant today, but four or five could pop up next year.

SEDGE

Sedge is a common perennial that grows from three inches to three feet tall and ranges from six to 24 feet wide, depending on the variety and the environmental conditions. Sedge grows green, grass-like leaves in clumps, but it really isn't a grass. This plant requires little care and will grow and spread very quickly

Plant sedge in partial to full shade in moist to dry conditions. Cut it back after it blooms in autumn, leaving about two thirds of the plant's original height. Divide it in spring or summer.

SWITCHGRASS

Switchgrass is an ornamental perennial that stands tall with small flowers on its tips. It often appears naturally in prairies and savannahs in the Midwest and Eastern portions of the United States, growing best in zones five through nine. Since switchgrass is so widely adaptable, you can easily incorporate this rugged addition to your landscape. It makes a wonderful privacy screen, as well as a great back border.

There are many varieties of switchgrass. The Cloud Nine and North Wind varieties will grow from five to six feet in height with little horizontal spread. Its leaf is dark green and when it blooms in the summer, you will be treated to rich, deeply hued flowers. Dallas Blues will grow up to eight feet tall, producing purple leaves and two-inch seed heads. The Heavy Metal variety produces blue blades. Shenandoah switchgrass is a shorter variety that only grows two feet tall.

Before you plant switchgrass, carefully plan its location. If you use it as a garden border, plant your switchgrass so it doesn't shade or block smaller plants. This ornamental grass looks great planted along a fence or in your front yard as a privacy screen. Plant your switchgrass in groups that are at least one foot apart.

This plant prefers full sun, but can tolerate a bit of shade. It grows best in soil that is loamy, sandy, or clay-like and will tolerate moist soil. Add compost to the planting site and set it in the ground at the same height it was in its original pot. Mulching will slow down its spread.

Switchgrass is a wonderfully low-maintenance plant. If your soil is extremely poor, you'll want to apply some fertilizer in the spring, but otherwise, it is maintenance-free. I also recommend keeping the surrounding area free of weeds by keeping the soil around it rich with organic matter. Divide switchgrass every couple of years, if you desire. This grass can be susceptible to fungal diseases, including leaf spots, crown rot, root rot, rust and smut. It can also be attacked by grasshoppers, aphids, chinch bugs, leaf hoppers, beetles, and wireworms. At the same time, it attracts beneficial creatures such as spiders, wasps and ants.

TUFTED HAIR GRASS

Tufted hair grass grows to between two and three feet tall and the same width. It sports green blades that turn yellow to bronze in the fall. Its flowers bloom from June to September, creating seed heads that turn green, brown, and gold in the fall. This grass loves moist soil and partial shade; it grows well by streams or ponds. It is used frequently as an erosion preventative.

Set the plants in spring or summer, allowing at least four feet all around for growth. Old leaves will turn brown; you'll want to remove them periodically. Do not fertilize this plant. Just put a few inches of compost around it every spring.

PERENNIAL SHRUBS

AZALEA

Azaleas are woody shrubs with small oval green leaves and magnificent flowers that bloom in the spring. The bush will be filled entirely with bell-shaped blooms in yellow, orange, purple, red, or pink. The shrubs grow anywhere from two to 10 feet tall, depending on the variety and the local climate. They prefer partial shade and rich soil with a bit of acidity. Full sun can actually burn the leaves.

There are two types of azaleas. The evergreen azalea stays green year round and grows in zones five to eight. The deciduous form loses its leaves for the winter and thrives in zones four to nine.

Plant azaleas outdoors in the spring, after adding plenty of compost to the area. Cover the roots with mulch to retain moisture and to minimize weeds. Fertilizer is only necessary, should the plant exhibit stunted growth or the leaves turn yellow and curl.

Azaleas require light pruning to maintain their shape and fullness. Trim after the flowers have finished blooming.

BLEEDING HEART

The Bleeding heart is a delicate perennial that requires full shade. Its foliage is green and rounded with heart-shaped leaves. Heart-shaped flowers drip down from thin arching stems in white, pink, red, or yellow. The bleeding heart blooms only in the spring, except for in cool climates, where it has been known to bloom throughout the summer. It grows well in zones four to eight and is deer resistant. This miniature shrub grows anywhere from five inches to two feet in height, depending on the variety you've planted.

Transplant bleeding heart into well-drained soil that has been amended with a great deal of organic matter. Mulch it to keep the roots cool. Every spring, add two inches of compost and additional mulch. After the first hard frost, cut them back to one inch above the ground, then mulch for the winter.

BUTTERFLY BUSH

Butterfly bushes are shrub perennials that attract butterflies as well as birds with their fruity fragrance. They grow quickly and their shoots can extend as high as eight feet. Their huge blossoms of spiky flowers in yellow, purple, pink, white, or red easily overwhelm their green foliage. Butterfly bushes grow best in zones five to 10 and they bloom both summer and fall, giving you – and the critters they attract – plenty of time to enjoy their beauty.

Butterfly bushes require full sunlight and thrive in fertile-well drained soil. Plant them in the spring or the fall. Do not over-fertilize to avoid stunting the leaf growth. Deadhead the spent flowers to encourage long-lasting blooms. Each spring, cover the roots with a small amount of compost and mulch to help retain moisture and control weed growth. If you live in a cold region, add a thicker layer of mulch in the fall, to help the bush weather the winter. Cut butterfly bushes back every spring to encourage blooming on new growth.

Butterfly bushes are susceptible to caterpillars, spider mites, weevils, and capsid bugs. They may also yield to fungal leaf spot, but are resistant to deer. The most popular varieties of butterfly bush are Petite Indigo and White Fusion.

FLOWERING QUINCE

The flowering quince is a shrub that produces beautiful flowers, and sometimes a little fruit, in early spring. It is native to Asia but appeared in home gardens all over the world by the 1800s. Flowering quince have twisted and thorny branches that grow up to five feet tall. Many people plant multiple quince bushes together to create a natural fence.

These plants bloom in the very early spring, around March. The blooms will grow to about the size of a nickel and can vary in color from orange to pink. The plant may also grow a pear-like tart fruit if the previous winter was not too harsh.

Flowering quince grows best in zones five to nine. It requires full sun but a little shade is tolerated. They thrive in well-drained sandy or clay soil. Apply a thick layer of mulch at the base of the plant to help preserve moisture and eliminate weeds. Unless you experience inadequate rainfall in your area, you won't need to water your quince regularly. Apply a nitrogen-based fertilizer each spring.

The most common varieties of flowering quince are Texas Scarlet, Cameo, Jet Trail and Toyo Nishiki. Texas Scarlet lives up to its name with bright red flowers. Cameo produces double pink blooms. Jet Trail only grows three feet tall, but it produces beautiful white flowers. Toyo Nishiki yields variegated blooms.

FORSYTHIA

Forsythia is a flowering shrub that blooms in early spring. The four-lobed brilliant yellow flowers appear before the leaves, which are small and oval-shaped; they look beautiful the rest of the season against the gray brown bark of the shrub. Forsythia grows well in full sun and partial shade in well-drained soil that is amended with organic matter every spring. Use mulch to retain moisture around the roots because this shrub requires about two inches of rainfall each week. Prune it after the blooms have faded, just to keep the bush under control. Otherwise, it has a tendency to sprawl all over the place. Forsythia works well as a background bush or, when well trained, as a hedge.

GARDENIA

Gardenias are ornamental shrubs with small flowers and a pleasant fragrance. The only drawback is that they are native to the South and do not handle winter at all. On the upside, dedicating your time and resources to proper gardenia care can yield fabulous results.

Gardenias grow best in regions with warm winters. They prefer partial shade and moist, well-drained acidic soil mixed with organic matter. Gardenias require regular watering and it is important to prune them after they finish blooming, to keep the plants healthy and strong. Gardenias do not fare well in cool climates, but pruning can help them survive mild southern winters a little easier.

Keep your gardenias healthy with frequent fertilization. The optimal time to fertilize is between early spring and early fall. Use a fertilizer that is suited for acidic plants. Be careful to follow the package instructions to avoid potential salt damage caused by over-fertilization.

HYDRANGEA

Hydrangeas have large ruffled leaves and yield impressive balls of flowers in white, pink or blue, depending on the plant variety and the soil's pH. They grow from two to six feet tall and spread from three to 10 feet wide. As the name would imply, hydrangeas need a great deal of water, about two inches of water per week.

Plant this shrub in a shady spot in the spring or fall, mulching the roots well to retain moisture. The plants will need to be spaced between three and nine feet apart, depending on the variety. Some hydrangeas form buds on old wood and must be pruned back after the flowers fade. Others form buds on new wood; these varieties require pruning before they bloom in the spring. Fertilize the hydrangea only in late winter or early spring, never during the summer.

It is important to protect hydrangeas from the cold of winter. Build a ring of chicken wire around the entire shrub, if possible and fill it with leaves, straw or pine needles to keep it snug and warm during the winter. Remove everything in the spring after the last frost.

LILAC

Lilacs are a perennial shrub that produces broad, dark green leaves and beautiful, sweet-smelling flower clumps. Depending on the variety, the color of the flowers will be blue, white, pink, or red. The most common variety of lilac blooms only for two weeks in May, but other varieties will bloom for up to six weeks. Lilacs are easy to grow and care for. They thrive in zones three to seven and typically bloom between March and June.

Lilacs require three to six hours of sun daily and prefer fertile soil with excellent drainage and a pH of approximately 7.0. You can successfully grow lilacs in poor soil as long as you mix in some compost. Plant your lilacs, preferably, in the fall, although spring planting is not out of the question. The planting process for lilacs is almost ridiculously easy. Just plant an offshoot or sucker, cover it with soil and water well. Although it will take several years to become established, you will eventually have a shrub that can grow between five and 15 feet tall and yield a profusion of colorful, aromatic blooms. Space the individual plants five to 15 feet apart, depending on the variety. If you want blooms earlier than May, just purchase a container plant and plant it in early fall.

Caring for lilacs is relatively easy. Apply a thin layer of compost to each shrub in the spring to help retain moisture and prevent weeds. If the summer in your region is very dry, water your lilacs regularly. If the shrub grows too wide, trim it back. The best time to prune lilacs is immediately following their spring bloom. They form buds on old wood so it is important to prune them as soon after the bloom has faded as possible.

Lilacs are generally targeted by slugs and snails. They can also host powdery white mildew, but this will not damage the plant.

MOCK ORANGE

Mock orange bushes grow from three to 15 feet tall and about six feet wide. They get their name from the fragrant flowers, which look like orange blossoms. The mock orange blooms for about a week in late spring. The foliage is a pleasant dark green.

The mock orange grows in zones four through eight in full sun to partial shade in moist soil with a good deal of compost added every spring. The shrub is relatively drought tolerant but does need some mulch to keep the roots cool and moist. Fertilize it in late winter or early spring if its growth slows.

Prune the mock orange after it blooms. The blossoms actually form in the fall, so spring pruning would destroy the blooms.

ROSE OF SHARON

The rose of Sharon grows up to 12 feet tall with green leaves and huge flowers resembling a hibiscus in white, pink, red and purple. These blooms keep going all summer long.

This bush, a form of hydrangea, is virtually indestructible. It grows in the worst soils and under the worst conditions. The shrubs can be shaped individually or you can plant them about two feet apart and shape them to serve as a hedge or screen. The rose of Sharon will re-seed, so you may easily find little bushes sprouting randomly in the spring. Plant in full sun or partial shade, adding compost in spring and mulching around the roots.

Flowers form on the new growth, so if you need to prune rose of Sharon, do so before the leaves and blooms set on in early spring.

SPIREA

Spirea is a delightful shrub, with its cascading streams of flowers in white, blue, pink, or red that sprout on arching stems with small green leaves. The bush grows up to 10 feet tall and blooms in spring and summer. Flowers come first and then narrow, green leaves that turn yellow and drop off in the fall.

Spirea does well in full sun to light shade, but needs full sun to bloom. Mulch the bush to keep water in the roots. Prune it after the bloom fades.

VIBURNUM

Viburnum bushes have the most fragrant flowers of the spring. Some varieties have purplish-red leaves while others are blue green. Little clusters of flowers are in pink, white, blue or yellow and they turn into berries that start out green and progress to pink, yellow, red, blue or black. The shrub grows from five to 15 feet.

Plant in spring, spacing seeds or starts five to 15 feet apart. Water plants when dry; mulch around the base of the plant to retain the moisture. Viburnum does not normally require fertilization, but it does benefit from a few inches of compost placed around the roots every spring.

Prune any time after it flowers. Some varieties can be cut back in winter or early spring.

YUCCA

Yuccas are popular perennials that are widely used for landscaping. They are easy to maintain and very tolerant of drought periods, making them a great addition to your garden.

Yuccas have rugged, sword-like foliage with tiny white flowers that tower above the foliage and emit a pleasant smell. Yucca plants are native to the Southwestern United States and both Central and South America. They thrive in rocky deserts and subtropical regions. In the United States, they can be grown in zones three to 10.

Yuccas require full sun, although a little shade is tolerable. Well-drained, average soil is best for yucca plants. If you can plant them on a slope, all the better for drainage; too much sustained moisture can lead to root rot.

To transplant yucca, dig a hole that is double the depth of the root ball. Space the plants at least three feet apart to allow for growth. Add sand or gravel to some soil, to obtain a fifty-fifty mix.

Stir in a little organic matter. Add a few inches of the soil mixture to the bottom of the hole, then set the root ball in the hole before filling it up with the mixture. Fill the hole until the soil is even with the ground. Water the yucca, but then leave it alone for a couple of weeks. Yucca plants generally bloom from mid-summer to mid-autumn.

FOLIAGE PLANTS

Foliage plants add a little more definition to your garden beds. They fill in where there may be empty spots and lend fullness to the garden. You can use perennial foliage plants as ground cover, filler, or as spectacular focus plants.

ARTEMESIA

Artemisia is best known for its silvery foliage. In addition to a striking appearance, artemesia is used in cooking and as a medicinal herb. One variety, Silver Mounds, is used for borders and as edging. It is a non-invasive spreading plant with fine, delicate leaves that form into mounds. The plant is very heat tolerant and is actually at its best in the middle of a hot summer. Since Silver Mounds does not grow very tall, it is considered a form of ground cover.

Artemesia requires full sun with a little afternoon shade and grows well in average soil. If your soil is too poor or too rich it can prevent the plant from reaching full maturity; the mound may split and die. By dividing artemesia plants at least every couple of years, you help promote their health, even if your soil is outside of the normal range.

You do not have to water artemesia regularly; only if your area experiences little to no rainfall. You can trim the plant during the middle of the summer and water it at that time. Artemesia are resistant to deer and other pests, so it can serve as a great protection for other plants.

FERNS

Ferns are perennials with feathery textured, fine foliage. They grow well in moist, shaded conditions. There are over 20,000 varieties of fern; some are considered evergreen while others die down in the fall and return in the spring. Ferns require shade and well-drained soil. Too much sunlight can scorch their leaves. Ferns grow between one and six feet tall; most spread broadly. When planting, it helps to add compost into the digging holes, You'll want to cover the soil with a thick layer of organic matter upon planting and then yearly thereafter. Water well and keep the plant watered consistently.

This plant does well in zones four through nine, although different varieties' requirements vary somewhat. The Japanese Painted Fern has silver fronds on burgundy stems that grow 12 to 18 inches tall and two to four feet wide. Feathery green foliage is the hallmark of the Ostrich fern, the largest fern variety, as well as the Fancy Fern, one of the most common types of fern.

LADY'S MANTLE

The lady's mantle provides great ground cover that grows best in partial shade, but can tolerate quite a bit of sun. It has gray green semi-circular leaves that are scalloped to grow to between six and 12 inches in diameter. The plant produces tiny chartreuse flowers in late spring and may bloom into midsummer. Lady's mantle spreads by self-seeding, so give it room to expand.

Before planting, add about two inches of compost to the area and dig down about six inches to loosen the soil. Set your plants eight to 12 inches apart. The leaves are green even in winter, but some may die back and turn brown. Just remove the brown leaves and in the spring you will have an abundance of pretty new foliage.

LAMB'S EARS

Kids love lamb's ears because of their fuzzy, velvet-like texture; the soft green leaves actually do look like lamb's ears. This plant is virtually indestructible and might be hard to get rid of if you ever decide you don't want it anymore. It grows well in zones four to eight, with leaves alternating up a stem. It produces stalks bearing pretty little pink or purple flowers during the summer that attract bees like crazy.

Lamb's ears do not need much encouragement to grow. Just give them a bit of compost after planting and more every spring. The plant likes full sun but grows fairly well in partial shade. They will spread, so give them room to grow and space the plants one foot apart. They may look sparse the first year, but will fill in rather rapidly. If you do not want them to spread, cut off the flower stalks right after they bloom. During the winter, some of the leaves may die back and turn brown. Just remove the dead leaves and they will be replaced quickly in the spring.

PACHYSANDRA

Pachysandra is an evergreen ground cover that produces small white to purple flowers in the spring. It grows well in zones four to seven and will tolerate very poor soil. It does not do well in full sun, so pachysandra must be planted in partial to full shade. The best location for this plant is beneath a big tree; it will provide ground cover around any protruding roots. If you create a box surrounding the tree and fill it with pachysandra, you will have an attractive focal point in your yard.

Space each plant six to 12 inches apart; they will soon cover the ground so all you'll see is a lush expanse of pachysandra. Pinch back new growth to encourage bushing. Water your pachysandra frequently; it needs one to two inches of water each week. Divide as needed to encourage healthy growth.

SNOW ON THE MOUNTAIN

This plant, also known as bishop's weed, is a wonderful ground cover. It can be invasive, so it needs to be controlled. Plant within edging sunk at least two inches below ground.

This plant gets its name from its appearance. The pretty green leaves have white edges that look like a touch of snow. Snowy white flowers appear in the spring.

Snow on the mountain grows best in zones three to nine and any type of soil will do, just as long as it is well-drained. This plant requires significant shade; the leaves will burn if it gets too much sun. Space your plants about a foot apart, because they will rapidly fill the area. They only need to be watered when dry. After the plants bloom, run over the area with a mower; they will soon pop back up, rejuvenated.

SOLOMON'S SEAL

Solomon's seal is a shade plant that works well as ground cover in zones three to seven. It has long ribbed green and variegated leaves that turn a pleasant yellow in the fall. The plant grows anywhere from 12 inches to two feet tall and produces pretty bell-shaped white flowers atop thin arching stems during late summer. The resulting brown to black berries appear shortly thereafter.

Plant Solomon's seal in soil that has been amended with compost. Space the plants two feet apart. Solomon's seal is somewhat drought tolerant. It prefers moist, but not wet soil. It spreads well and is easily divided to encourage new growth.

WORMWOOD

Wormwood displays pretty, frilly green leaves that resemble those of a marigold plant. It grows from one to three feet tall with an approximate two-foot spread. Striking yellow blooms appear in summer; you'll want to remove them before they are spent to maintain the plant's appearance. Plant in full sun to partial shade, in well-drained soil amended with compost. Space them one to three feet apart and they will fill in quickly.

Chapter 4: Perennial Bulbs and Rhizomes

Some perennials grow from bulbs, underground onion-like structures. These spring perennial bulbs are mostly planted in the fall before the ground begins to freeze for winter.

Rhizomes are another form of "seed" for some perennials. They look like a fat plant root with additional roots growing out from it. The rhizome is actually a horizontal plant stem that grows underground, propagating sideways, even as it sends roots downward. While bulbs usually bloom in the spring, rhizomes will often bloom all summer long.

ALLIUM

The allium, or ornamental onion, can add unique texture to your garden. It has large leaves at the base of a very long single stalk that supports a globe-shaped group of tiny flowers. The blooms can range anywhere from one to three feet tall, depending on the variety. This makes it a desirable choice for background border; the bright color without surrounding greenery really pops in front of a contrasting fence or wall.

Alliums grow in zones three to nine, also depending on the strain. They will thrive in almost any quality of soil, but it must be well drained to avoid root rot. Plant in fall and give the large roots plenty of room to grow. You will want to thin your alliums every few years to keep the blooms large and healthy.

As its nickname implies, the allium is related to the onion. It has a strong flavor that deer – and most mammals – find offensive.

ANEMONE/WINDFLOWER

Anemones are basic, flowering perennials that have long, leafy stems and bloom in an array of colors from white to green.

Anemones are native to rocky regions in the Mediterranean. They bloom in either the fall or the spring, depending on their variety. Anemones are poisonous if consumed, but have been used to treat tuberculosis and bone fractures. Anemones are a delightful addition to your rock gardens or flower bed.

Spring-blooming anemones grow from rhizomes while fall blooming types grow from a tuberous root. It is helpful to pre-soak the rhizomes or roots overnight before planting them between one and two inches deep. Anemones require full to partial sun and they thrive in rich, well-drained loamy soil. It can be helpful to add compost and rotted manure to the planting site prior to planting. Water anemones regularly; just don't waterlog the soil. Apply a general fertilizer once a month. Once they are established, deadhead the blooms to keep them producing flowers. Allow them to die back naturally and they will reappear next growing season. Mulch the surrounding soil to retain moisture and minimize weeds. Anemones can be susceptible to slugs, beetles, and aphids as well as fungal diseases.

CROCOSMIA

Crocosmia, a member of the iris family, is a flowering perennial bulb with origins that trace back to South America. The flowers are shaped like clusters of tiny iris, and appear in colors of red, orange, and yellow. Crocosmia plants bloom between late summer and mid-fall. They are hardy in zones five to nine.

Crocosmia plants grow between two to five feet tall. It is best to plant the bulbs in the fall for spring blooms. Plant the bulbs, or corms, two to three inches deep and about eight to 10 inches apart. After a couple of years, you can divide the bulbs in the fall.

Crocosmia requires full sun and thrives in loose, rich and well-drained soil. If your current soil doesn't have good drainage, add in some sand. It is important to keep Crocosmia watered and give it a regular application of fertilizer. When the plants die back in the fall, cut them back to ground level. If you live in a region that experiences low winter temperatures, apply a large amount of mulch to prevent frost damage.

CROCUS

The crocus is one of the first flowers to bloom in spring. It grows low to the ground, but is hard to overlook with its vividly colored flowers, especially when it sprouts amid snow. The entire plant only stands two to four inches tall, but it makes up for its diminutive size with brightly colored blooms. The crocus flower is small, goblet-shaped, and vivid purple, yellow-orange, white, or blue with a bright yellow stamen. The Pickwick variety has striped dark and light petals with a purple base. The Tri-color crocus sports bands of white, gold, and lilac. The earliest bloomer is the Dutch crocus, with solid bright colors reminiscent of the tulips of Holland.

Crocus require more shade than sun. They do well when set in clusters of 10 or more. Plant your tiny crocus bulbs in the fall before the ground begins to freeze, adding compost to the hole. The bulbs should be set three to four inches deep, with the pointed end up. Cover the bulbs with a thick cushion of mulch for the winter in cold zones, but remember to remove the covering in late February or Early March.

DAFFODIL

Daffodils are easy to grow; they tolerate harsh weather and grow almost anywhere in the United States. Daffodils produce golden, 6-lobed yellow blooms with a petal crown center. Along with crocus, the daffodil marks the start of spring.

Daffodils have thick blade-like leaves and put up a long stem on which the flower grows. Some varieties grow clusters of flowers. Daffodil blooms are not limited to yellow. Some varieties produce white blooms; others produce crowns of yellow, orange, pink, or green. The center crowns can be simple or ruffled and can be

66

solid in color or rimmed with a contrasting shade. Many gardeners use daffodils as border plants. They also grow well between shrubs or under trees in a natural setting.

The cut flowers are fairly durable and will add a touch of spring indoors. Just don't combine daffodils with other flowers; their sap contains a substance that causes other flowers to wilt.

Daffodils grow best in zones three to nine. Planting them in the early fall will establish them for blooming as soon as the soil warms above freezing. Daffodils need full sunlight with little shade. They grow best in loamy, slightly acidic fertile soil that is well drained. Daffodils are grown from large bulbs.

Plant the bulbs twice as deep as their bulb is tall, with the pointed end up. Add a little fertilizer in the planting hole. Cover the bulb for the winter with at least four inches of soil for maximum protection. It is best to space your daffodils three to six inches apart, but they appear natural in clusters of five or more.

If the growing conditions in the spring are dry, water your daffodils. In the fall, the leaves and stems will wither and turn yellow, but do not cut them back until they are completely dry. This gives enough time for the energy of the plant to sink into the bulb, allowing it to emerge strong and healthy the next spring. As their flowers fade, deadhead them to enhance the appearance of your plants.

Daffodils are most susceptible to bulb flies, bulb mites, nematodes, slugs, plant viruses and fungal infections. The most recommended varieties of daffodil are Golden Ducat, Petit Four, and Rip van Winkle.

GRAPE HYACINTH

Grape hyacinths are another spring blooming favorite that is small, dainty, and close to the ground at about four inches tall.

Their name comes from their blooms, which look like an upside down cluster of miniature purple grapes.

Grape hyacinth bulbs are very small and must be planted in the fall. This plant loves full sun to partial shade and dry soil. Plant the small bulbs twice as deep as the bulb is tall and two to three inches apart. These flowers appear natural when planted in clusters of five or more.

HYACINTH

Hyacinths are perennial flowers, native to the Mediterranean, that bear a lovely fragrance and can be an excellent addition to your therapeutic garden. Hyacinths grow best in zones five to nine and are best planted in the fall to anticipate spring flowers. The first blooming of a hyacinth will yield condensed, bell-shaped flowers on a 10-inch tall plant. Hyacinths require full sun and are best grown from bulbs. Plant your bulbs three times as deep as their height. It can be helpful to plant a stake near your hyacinths to support the first year's heavy flowers. The flowers, depending on the variety, are pink, blue, white, dark purple, or yellow. You will continue to water the plants after the flowers have withered away.

Note: Hyacinths can aggravate sensitive skin, so it is recommended to wear gloves while handling this plant.

IRIS

The quantity of iris varieties is astounding. and one of the most popular is the Dutch, or bearded, iris. Most varieties are about 28 inches high although some are much smaller and have flat leaf blades in green to gray or blue green. The flower has three large outer petals calls falls and three inner upright petals called standards. The falls often have hairy beards or crests. Most iris varieties bloom early summer and need full sun to produce flowers. Iris flowers can be one color or many and come in almost all the colors of the rainbow.

Plant iris rhizomes in late summer after mixing about two inches of compost into the soil. Plant single rhizomes or place them in groupings of three to five. The rhizome of irises is never completely buried; some of it should protrude aboveground.

Iris plants are drought and deer resistant and most varieties grow well in zones four to nine.

The Siberian iris is just as popular as the Dutch or Bearded iris.

SIBERIAN IRIS

Siberian irises are easy to grow, easy to spot perennials that bear green spiky and erect leaves with blooms of various colors including red, yellow, orange, white, pink, violet and blue. Some blooms may bear multicolored flowers while others may bloom in only one hue. Many people use Siberian irises to border their gardens or other areas of their property. Siberian irises bloom from the mid-spring to early summer and grow best in zones four to nine.

Siberian irises require full sunlight with a little shade. They grow between two and three feet tall and one to one ½ feet wide. Siberian irises prefer well-drained soil with a high level of fertility. It is best to plant Siberian irises from rhizomes, which you should obtain between the summer and the fall. The tops of the rhizomes should be just below ground level when you plant them. It is helpful to apply a fertilizer that is low in nitrogen upon your initial planting and then apply it again during the spring. You'll know when to divide the plants when overcrowding begins to occur.

In terms of pests, Siberian irises are most susceptible to aphids, nematodes, iris borers, slugs and snails, whiteflies and thrips. In terms of disease, Siberian irises are most susceptible to leaf blight, bacterial soft rot, leaf spot, rhizome rot and crown rot. Siberian irises may keep deer away from your property and they can serve as cut flowers.

LILY

Lilies are colorful and pleasant-smelling perennials with large, trumpet-shaped flowers and tall, rigid stems. They are easy to grow as long as you carefully consider their growing site. Lilies bloom between the spring and fall and are best grown in zones four to eight. Some common varieties include old fashioned orange and brown tiger lilies, Hemerocallis lilies in all shades of yellow and gold, orange and red to pink and hybrid lilies from pale pink to chartreuse, nearly black, purple and white.

Choosing the right growing site for lilies is the most important consideration for planting lilies. Lilies require between six and eight hours of full sun per day. Too much shade can cause the flowers to droop. Lilies also require very well-drained soil that is acidic to neutral. Add organic compost to the soil to encourage better drainage. It is important to loosen the soil to about a foot or more into the earth. This gives the roots room to grow and establish themselves. Plant the bulbs two times as deep as the height of the bulb. Space the bulbs three times the distance of their diameter. Water bulbs after you plant them and then mulch them to help retain moisture. Afterwards, they should not need much more watering unless you experience little rainfall.

Apply a liquid fertilizer to lilies every month, beginning in the spring up until six weeks after they flower. Add a small amount of compost followed by mulch. Cut back dead stems in the winter and divide the plants ever couple of years. Lilies are most susceptible to gray mold and viruses spread by aphids. They may also fall victim to slugs, snails or small mammals.

LILY OF THE VALLEY

Lily of the Valley is a low growing semi to full shade plant that is often natural on a forest floor. The plant grows from small bulbs and has flat green lance shaped leaves that droop and tiny white, bell-shaped flowers that drip from thin stems that are very fragrant. They only grow four to eight inches high and about three to five inches wide. They are most comfortable growing in zones two to nine in moist soil. Plant during late fall as they need a dormant cold period to bloom. Divide lily of the valley bulbs after they flower in the spring.

SNOWDROP/GALANTHUS

These little gems grow only in cold regions and they bloom when the snow is still in the flower beds in late February and March. The plant will not grow in the south because they need a cold dormant period. The plants grow about four to six inches high and have green leaves much like miniature dafodil leaves with white or pink drooping trumpet-like flowers.

Snowdrops grow from what are called green bulbs. These are bulbs that have not dried like daffodil or tulip bulbs and they must be planted immediately or they will dry out and not sprout. Ammend soil with compost and dig down to soften the dirt so roots can dig down easily. Plant with the point up on the bulb in soil one to two to six inches deep and three inches apart. Plant bulbs in groups of 10 to 25.

TULIP

Tulips are another spring blooming flower that have basically the same shape, but their petals have some differences. The flower is usually goblet shaped with either smooth or ragged petals. They grow about a foot or two high with thick, flat green leaves at the bottom of the tall skinny stem and the flower sitting on top. The colors are endless and they are solid colors all the way to many different colors. Tulips are perennials in the north where there is a cold dormant time for the bulbs and in the south they are

71

treated as annuals. They bloom for three to four weeks in the spring.

Plant bulbs point up two times the depth of the height of the bulb about six to eight weeks before a hard frost. Amend the soil with plenty of compost prior to planting. Tulips like dry soil and do not tolerate soggy situations where the bulb can easily rot. Add unscented kitty litter in the hole before inserting the bulb to deter rhodents from digging them up. Those that have squirell problems may have to plant the bulbs in wire cages. Rhodents find tulip bulbs a delicacy. Tulips insist on full sun in order to bloom well.

Space them three to six inches apart and plant in clusters so they look natural. Deadhead the flower heads once they start to die back, but never cut back the stem and leaves even though they turn yellow and look ugly. The leaves have to be dried and brown before they are removed because the process of dying back is what gives energy to the bulb so that it can bloom again next year. If you cut it back, the bulb may not have enough energy to put forth a flower in the spring again. Braid the leaves and secure them with a rubber band leaving them to lie on the garden floor. Once they dry just pull and they should come off easily. Mulch tulips to retain moisture and add compost around the planting bed early spring

Chapter 5: Perennial Herbs Add Flavor To Life

Most herbs are perennials, which is fortunate because there is so much you can do with them. In addition to spicing up foods, they can be used as natural health remedies or in cleaning solutions. Some herbs will enhance the health of other plants or serve as natural insect repellants for your garden plants. They can enhance your flower gardens and add color and texture to your landscaping, so don't assume they must be relegated to the vegetable garden plot.

Most perennial herbs are best started using container plants; some do not start well from seeds. Some grow from cuttings but it can be a little complicated to persuade them to root if you aren't an expert at the process. Most herbs enjoy full sun, but a few do well in partial shade. If you plan to use your herbs for cooking or other preparations, you will want to prevent them from blooming The flower signifies the end of the growing season and shuts down the plant. Instead, you want to cut the plant and either dry or freeze the useful leaves. This will allow the plant to regrow so you can reap another harvest.

What follows are some perennial herbs that I would recommend for use in either an herb garden or with other plants in your yard.

CHIVES

Chives are a very versatile herb plant that looks nice in borders or just as a plant in an herb garden. It presents itself as a mound of long, skinny green blades in green to blue green with big purple to lavender pompon-like flowers appearing on thin stems. Both the leaves and the flowers have a mild onion flavor.

Chives require a cold period to grow, so they are treated as an annual in the south. Those lucky people up north can expect a chive plant to grow for many years. Chives require full sun to partial shade. They generally do not need to be fertilized and will grow in even the poorest soil, but the soil has to be well drained. If the plants are not performing well, fertilize with a granular 20-20-20 fertilizer once a month placed around the base of the plant, scratched into the soil and watered in. Chives are drought tolerant and should only be watered when the soil is dry.

Chives grow from little bulbs beneath the soil and they multiply every year. Planting by seeds can take forever to get a plant that will produce, so it is better to plant from a container plant or from a transplant from a friend's garden. Just dig a hole deep enough to contain the cluster of bulbs and cover them completely. Space plants eight to 12 inches apart.

Clip chives at will or harvest by cutting ½ inch above the soil. This may be done as soon as the plant reaches about eight inches high. The leaves will soon start to grow again and you can harvest again when the leaves reach eight inches high. To keep the plant producing, cut off the flowers. These flowers are edible. After the first frost, chive leaves will turn brown and die back. Cut them back to about two inches above the ground and mulch for winter. Divide chives in early spring

GARLIC CHIVES

Garlic chives are tasty, cool-season herbs that belong to the onion family. They are a must-have for any garden. Garlic chives are used for the flower as well as an herb to add flavor to soups and stews. While regular chives have an onion flavor, the flavor of both garlic and onion are combined in garlic chives. This plant can help your garden look amazing and when you're ready, you can harvest them for use in recipes.

Deer hate garlic chives, so including them in your garden can keep Bambi away with minimal effort. The plants are also evergreen and extremely easy to care for. Garlic chives grow up to 24 inches tall and blossom in the late spring, all summer long and in the early fall. Garlic chives commonly bear pinkish purple flowers but they can also be red, violet, pink or white in color. Cut the flowers and use them as decoration and they also bear a wonderful smell.

Garlic chives grow best in zones three through nine. They prefer full sun with a little shade. This plant grows best in acidic, damp soil. Aim for a soil pH of 6.2 to 6.8 when planting.

While garlic chives grow well in a traditional in-ground garden, they tend to grow especially well in rock features and container gardens. Plant garlic chives either in the spring or fall. It takes approximately one to three weeks for the seeds to germinate, but you can save the seeds for up to three years. It will take quite some time for you to be able to harvest garlic chives if planted by seed. If you are in a hurry, purchase container plants and space them eight to 12 inches apart.

The best way to keep your plants healthy is to cut them back regularly. Cutting garlic chives will also help them spread throughout your garden. It is best to divide the flowers and replant them in new soil every three to five years. The best news of all is that garlic chives are normally invulnerable to pests and disease!

LAVENDER

Lavender is a favorite plant in France; it provides a popular fragrance utilized in the perfume industry. Lavender has a clean, fresh scent that comes from bud-like purple flowers and from the short, needle-like blue-green leaves. Lavender is easily grown in an herb or flower garden. It tends to grow like a shrub, with woody stems. It is especially beautiful when clipped into a hedge. The flowers appear above the foliage on tall stems. If the stems are cut as long as possible and the flowers are bundled and hung to dry, they emit a beautiful fragrance throughout your home.

Lavender does not grow easily from seed, so it is best to have a container plant or transplant from a friend's garden. You will want to plant it in the spring, after all danger of frost is past. Set the plants 12 to 18 inches apart in areas of full sun and well-drained soil. Lavender enjoys slightly alkaline soil, but will grow in almost anything. The plant blooms in late spring but can also flower again late summer for a second harvest. For best results, cut the flowers before they open fully.

Established plants need to be pruned during the spring. Get rid of any dead wood that does not green up in the spring. Even out the branches to make a pleasing presentation. Sprinkle some bone meal around the roots in the fall and dig it in to the soil. This will facilitate blooming the next year. Mulch heavily before winter to protect the roots from cold temperatures.

LEMON BALM

Lemon balm has a strong lemony scent with a hint of mint; it looks much like a mint plant, but the leaves are significantly larger. The green leaves spiral up to 24 to 36 inches tall on square stems. The plant does spread, but much slower than mint, because it reseeds from the pretty white flowers that grow on spikes above the foliage. These flowers also attract bees and other pollinators to the garden. You can cut the plant back to use in salads or dry the leaves to add to your tea. Lemon balm is easily dried by hanging the stalks upside down. The flavor does not last long when dried, but the fragrance endures, making it a good candidate for inclusion in potpourri.

Lemon balm is not picky about where it grows. It only asks for full sun and well-drained soil. Add a little compost to the site before planting starts 20 to 24 inches apart. Add more compost every spring to refresh the soil. Lemon balm aggressively reseeds from its own white flowers, so it is adviseable to pinch off the blooms before they all produce seed.

MARJORAM

Marjoram is a low-growing perennial herb that does well as ground cover or an edging plant. In zones nine and 10 it is a perennial, but it is questionable whether the plant will survive in colder areas. It grows small greenish gray oval leaves and produces small knot-like flowers that range from white to lavender. The plant grows from 12 to 14 inches tall.

Plant your starts after any danger of frost is past. Set the plants 12 inches apart in full sun, in soil that has been amended with compost. Marjoram rarely needs fertilizing but a shot of slow release fertilizer in the hole when planting will not do it any harm. Cut off the flowers before they totally open, in order to keep the plant growing and the flavor of the leaves true.

Bring the plant inside if you live in a cold climate or mulch it heavily. Marjoram prefers a dry climate. Pick the leaves as needed or harvest 1/3 of the plant during late summer and during spring for established plants. The flavor is retained when the leaves are dried, but the stems can also be frozen to capture the taste.

MINT

Mint is a popular herb with a distinct fragrance that is a popular recipe ingredient as well as a popular ice cream flavor. It's a good starter herb if you're new to herbology. The only drawback to growing mint is that it can easily take over your garden, it grows that easily. The plant propagates by spreading its roots underground but it can be contained by sinking two to 3-inch metal or plastic edging into the ground all around the plant. The runners will not be able to penetrate the barrier and will stay put. Another way to contain the plant is to remove the bottom from a plastic bucket and bury it so that only two inches is left standing out of the soil. Plant the mint plant in the middle of the bucket.

An ideal way to start mint is to buy a small mint plant (see important note at the end), although it is possible but difficult to start them from seeds. Once purchased, you should transplant the mint plant into a larger pot to allow it enough room to grow.

Mint needs lots of sunlight and water to thrive. Place the plant in full sun and well-drained soil. Never fertilize mint, because it already grows like a weed! Pinch off flowers so the plant remains tidy and flavor is not compromised.

To propagate a mint plant, cut off a sprig and place it in a cup of water until it sprouts roots. Small roots should appear on the sprigs after being in water for a week. When the roots are substantial enough, you can plant the sprigs in a new pot. Transfer the plants to the garden when they have at least three sets of leaves. As for eating it, mint is best used fresh, but the plant does retain scent and flavor when dried or frozen.

OREGANO

When you think of oregano, you most often think of Italian cooking, but oregano is also a favorite in Greek and Spanish cuisines. It is a Mediterranean perennial (Mexican oregano is a different taste altogether), that doesn't require much water but it does need at least six hours of sun per day. Oregano is a low-growing plant with small oval light green leaves that will cascade down a pot. Oregano usually grows four to five inches in height and five to 10 inches wide. It has a pungent flavor. It does well in pots as trailing plants, in an herb garden, or as edging. It produces little white flowers that should be pinched off to retain flavor in the leaves.

It grows best up to zone seven. Set container plants or seedlings in the ground in late spring, after the final frost. Space them 10 inches apart, since the plant will spread slightly. Oregano also grows well from cuttings. It is possible to start oregano from seed, but it must be started indoors about six to 10 weeks prior to the last frost of the season. You'll want to divide established plants in late spring. Water only when the soil beneath the plant is dry.

Cut back oregano at the end of spring to keep it bushy. Protect the plant during the winter with a thick layer of mulch. Be sure to remove it after the weather warms up a bit.

SAGE

What would Thanksgiving turkey be without sage stuffing? I protect my sage plants with a cage of chicken wire filled with dried leaves starting the end of September and it stays growing until after Thanksgiving so I can use the fresh herb in my stuffing. Sage has a pungent odor and flavor that mixes well with poultry and sausage. It grows in zones five to eight as a hardy perennial, but in the south it is considered an annual. It does not like extreme heat.

Sage is actually a low-growing shrub with woody branches and gray-green leaves that are soft and fuzzy. It grows about 12 to 30 inches tall, depending on the variety, and should be planted 18 to 24 inches apart. Sage loves full sun, well-drained soil and an occasional watering when it gets dry. If you have clay soil, just add a little sand and your sage will be fine.

It is very difficult to grow sage from seed so I recommend buying container plants or growing it from cuttings. The plant is also propagated by layering. You can layer the plant by taking a lower leaf and pinning it to the ground by the stalk, without removing it from the mother plant. I use press u-shaped pieces of wire over the stalk to secure it to the ground. Soon the leaf will sprout roots. Once you notice significant growth from the leaf, unpin it, dig it up and plant it in another location.

You'll want to prune your sage in the spring, getting rid of damaged branches and removing old wood that has become large and unproductive. At that time you can add mulch to keep the roots cool and to protect them during the winter. Replace the plants every five years if they become too woody.

Sage produces pretty purple to white flowers above the foliage. If you want the plant to keep growing and producing flavorful leaves, you'll want to pinch back these blooms. However, if you let it flower freely, the plant will be less productive but it will attract pollinators to the garden. Warning: do not plant sage near cucumbers; neither one will grow well.

SAVORY

There are two different types of savory. One is summer savory with a sweet flavor and is an annual plant and the other is winter savory that has a more robust flavor and is a perennial.

Winter savory is a bushy evergreen perennial with needle-like green leaves that grow about one inch long or shorter. The leaves grow on square stems that grow about one to two feet tall. The stems tend to get a little woody with age and need to be pruned every so often in the spring. The plant has small white to purple flowers growing on a spike.

This herb should be planted in full sun in soil that is a little dry. It is possible to start seeds indoors about eight weeks before the last anticipated frost of the season, but the seeds germinate very slowly and you will probably not have any harvest the first year. It is better to plant from container plants or transplants. Space your savory plants 12 to 18 inches apart.

Take cuttings at will. Wait until mid summer and cut the plant back to about a third of its full height. You can dry the leaves by hanging them in a shaded dry area. Once dry, strip the leaves from the stems and store in an airtight container. Cut off its flowers to keep the plant producing flavorful leaves. Every spring, add compost around the roots. It is recommended to replace old plants every four to five years.

TARRAGON

French tarragon is the herb to look for if you want fresh tarragon in your cooking. There is also a Mexican variety, but it is not as tasty. French tarragon looks like tall grass with slender light green leaves on long stalks. The stem grows to about 18 to 24 inches tall and the plant rarely produces flowers. It also does not spread or reseed. The only way to propagate this plant is via stem cuttings or divisions. The plant will go dormant in winter but will start up again as soon as the soil becomes warm in spring.

Tarragon prefers full sun, but will grow in partial shade. The plant does not grow from seeds. You'll want to start it from cuttings or container plants. Set them two to three feet apart in richly composted soil. Add compost every spring and mulch well in cold regions to protect the roots from freezing. Divide and replant every three to four years, in spring or fall.

YARROW

Yarrow is a hardy perennial that boasts fern-like, pleasant-smelling leaves and grows tiny and condensed flowers of white, pink, yellow, or red. Yarrow is easy to maintain and great for bordering gardens, lawns, or anything else around your property. Many people also use yarrow in rock configurations or wildflower gardens.

It grows best in zones three to nine. The Coronation Gold variety produces mustard-colored flowers with silver leaves. The Fanal variety produces deep red flowers with a yellow middle. The Cerise Queen produces blooms that are bright pink.

Yarrow requires at least six hours of sun and thrives in soil that is loamy or sandy, well-drained dry soil. I recommend loosening the soil up to a foot deep with a large amount of compost mixed in. It is best to plant container starts in the early spring.

Yarrow grows best in hot and dry conditions. If you're planting yarrow in rich soil, you may need to add in a support system, because this plant can grow between two and four feet tall and will often spread. Plant yarrow at least one foot apart.

Add a small amount of compost and a thick layer of mulch to your yarrow every spring. If you live in a region with minimal weekly rainfall, you'll want to water them regularly between June and August. It is best to divide yarrow every three to five years to keep the plants productive.

Chapter 6: Fruits and Berries

Berries are popular perennials that grow as plants in the ground, on bushes and trees or on canes, some of which have pretty trecherous thorns. They can grow wild and look like a mass of confusion, but if you take care of them, these berries can appear quite lovely in a garden. Some can be cut into hedges or can be formed into well-shaped bushes.

The greatest problem is that animals and birds are highly attracted to those blue, purple, or red berries. The critters can easily devour your fruit before you get a chance to harvest it! But we've foiled them! Newer varieties produce different colors – white, green, or yellow berries that are overlooked by wildlife but are every bit as tasty as the traditional varieties. You can also cover your berries with protective screens or cheesecloth to keep the berries all to yourself.

Most berries require an acidic soil with a pH of 5.5 to 6.0 whereas your vegetable garden would rather have a neutral soil pH of 7.0. For this reason, you'll want to plant your berries away from your vegetable and flower plots, but close enough to benefit from the bees and other pollinators they attract.

BLACKBERRIES

Blackberries are a popular berry that grows on the ends of perennial shrubs. Blackberries naturally grow in wooded areas, so they should be planted in partial shade and need soil with excellent drainage. They don't grow very well in clay soil but if you're not sure if your soil is proper for growing blackberries, mix organic matter into the soil to help promote aeration. Once you've selected your growing site, clear the soil of weeds, rocks and foreign objects. Add compost to the soil to make it rich. Begin planting blackberries as early as possible once the spring rolls around. Never plant them anywhere where tomatoes, eggplant or potatoes have been planted before.

Water blackberries immediately after planting them. If the starts are tall, cut them back half a foot after planting. New plants will not produce fruit for the first year. As long as you give them plenty of fertilizer and water, however, the plants should start to produce berries the second year. Starting the second year, add fertilizer in the spring and water once a week. Monitor the plants for weeds and pull any that appear. When the fruits have ripened, pick them every four to six days. With the proper care, your blackberry plants may produce fruit annually for up to 20 years.

BLUEBERRIES

Blueberries come in several varieties and it is necessary to start more than one variety for them to cross-pollinate and grow healthy fruit. If you want to pick blueberries all summer long, I recommend you plant several varieties, each one with a different fruit-bearing season.

Blueberries grow on pretty bushes that can make very nice hedges. Choose a site in full sun and work peat moss into the soil. Blueberries need acidic soil, so if the pH isn't between 5.0 and 6.0, you'll want to work some sulfur in to the area an entire season before you plant. It takes agricultural sulfur a whole year to do its job of changing alkaline or neutral soil to acidic.

Plant one- to three-year-old stock in your prepared soil. For each plant, dig a hole that is at least 20 inches deep and 18 inches wide. You'll want to space your blueberry plants five feet apart. Don't apply fertilizer when you first plant, but wait for a month before applying it.

In the fall, protect the roots of your bushes with mulch; add compost every spring. Blueberry bushes require about two inches of water per week and you'll probably want to cover them with netting if you don't want the birds to get all the berries.

Don't prune the bushes until they have grown in your garden for four years. Pruning is needed to stimulate growth after the third year. You'll want to prune your blueberries in late winter before any leaves appear.

CURRANTS

Currants are little round blackish-red berries that grow in clusters on bushes. They are very sour but make a great jelly. They can also be dried and used like raisins. Currant bushes require no maintenance at all. They are deer resistant, as well. They prefer full sun and well drained soil and benefit from a layer of mulch around the roots.

Most bushes will not bear fruit until they have been established for two or three years. Like blueberries, currant bushes benefit when you plant more than one variety, but they pollinate their own flowers, so it isn't necessary. Watch for restrictions on planting currants in your area; some places don't want the current bushes to carry a disease called White Pine Blister Rust to trees in the area, so they've been outlawed.

Currants grow in zones three to eight. They tend to drop their leaves if the temperature gets above 85 degrees Fahrenheit, but there are a few varieties that do tolerate hot temperatures. Plant them in acidic soil amended with plenty of compost by digging a hole so the plant sits at the same level it does in the container. Space the bushes four to five feet apart. Mulch around the roots and then water them about two inches per week. If you feel like you need to fertilize, use a 10-10-10 fertilizer once a year in the spring. Keep the chemical about a foot away from the roots. Currant bushes will generally produce berries for 15 to 20 years, with minimal pruning required. Cover them to protect the fruits from birds, unless you are growing one of the newer varieties that produce white berries, which birds are oblivious to.

MULLBERRIES

Mulberries are a small, sweet, and juicy berry that grows on trees, or in some cases bushes, in zones four to eight. They stain anything they fall on so I recommend planting them well away from any driveways, sidewalks, or deck surfaces. The trees can grow very large and require much room to grow. Their roots spread broadly.

Mulberries require full sun and soil amended with compost. They come in varieties that produce black, red, or white berries and birds love them. To plant, you'll want to dig a hole twice as wide as the root ball and as deep as the tree sits in its container. You will plant the start slightly higher than where it sat in the container. Space plants 30 to 50 feet apart.

RASPBERRIES

Raspberries tend to grow profusely, so it takes a bit of effort to tame the bushes and keep them looking nice. There are two basic types of raspberry, one that only produces berries only in the summer and an ever-bearing form that provides fruit from summer on into the fall. Raspberries grow thorny canes that tend to latch onto anything that passes by.

Plant your raspberry starts in the spring. Do not locate them near previous or current plantings of tomatoes, eggplant or potatoes. They require full sun and well drained soil. Begin by mixing several inches of compost into the soil. Dig a hole deep enough to accommodate the roots and space the plants three feet apart in rows eight feet apart. Raspberries love water, so soak the plants in water before planting and water them frequently until they establish themselves in the soil. Give them at least one inch of water per week and mulch the plants to retain moisture.

After a year, prune the older canes back, but leave the younger ones alone. In the fall, you'll want to prune them back, leaving about six of the best canes per plant. Do not let the plant grow any wider than 19 inches wide and cut off any canes that do not grow vertically.

STRAWBERRIES

Strawberries are a popular and refreshing fruit that just happens to be a perennial! The more active care you give your strawberries, the better they will taste when you can harvest them. Consequently, they make a great addition to a therapeutic garden.

You'll want to select your growing site in the spring. Look for a garden spot that will afford the plants complete sun. Work the soil thoroughly, turning a foot in depth before mixing in six inches of compost. For every 100 square feet, add two pounds of fertilizer.

Set your strawberry plants 18 to 24 inches deep. Each row of strawberry plants should be at least four feet apart. When you move the plant into the planting hole, place the tip of the crown barely above the soil. Spread out the roots, then carefully pack the soil around them. If you experience less than an inch of rainfall per week in your area, you will need to water your strawberry plants twice a week.

It is important to keep weeds away from strawberry plants. When you weed, be careful to avoid disturbing the roots. Watch especially for newly attached leaf clumps as the plant expands; their roots will be just beginning to grow. One month after planting, you can add an additional pound of fertilizer for every 100 square feet of plants. During the first growing season, you'll want to remove any blossoms that develop; yes, this will prevent berries from growing, but it will firmly establish the plant so that, next year, you will be able to enjoy luscious, large strawberries.

As cold weather approaches, add straw-based mulch around the plants to insulate and stabilize them. As soon as the chance of frost is past, discard down to a half inch of mulch as soon as you see leaves beginning to form.

Chapter 7: Landscaping With Perennials

When you think of the word "landscaping," you probably think about grass, hills, trees and other green elements that can make your front lawn or backyard beautifully appealing. However, don't forget that you can also improve your landscape with the judicious introduction of perennials. Trees, shrubs and flowering plants can be used to make bold statements on your property, or to create a secluded, private haven.

Perennials can add character to your yard and you can use them to express your personality. My grandmother, for example, has for decades nurtured an evergreen tree on the right side of her front lawn. It has become an iconic landmark of sorts. We can't picture her house without it!

The perennial landscaping possibilities are endless! There are so many varieties of perennial that choosing among them can be quite overwhelming. This chapter will help you wade through the multitude of options and come up with a landscaping plan that suits the contours of your property while answering well to your personal preferences.

GET THE LAY OF THE LAND

The first step is to take a good look at the area you have to work with. Observe your existing garden areas, noting the hills, rocks, valleys, and what is already growing there. Pay attention to how long the sun hits certain areas, how the soil drains and basically, what you have to work with.

SKETCH

The best way to get a handle on your land is to put it down on paper. You don't have to be fancy, nor do you need to be an artist. All you want is to be able to represent fairly accurately the lay of your land. Use grid paper if possible, allowing a set number

of squares to represent a single foot of the property you are landscaping. Mark existing features, including rocks, walls, buildings, fences, compost bins, sheds, and trellises. Indicate the spread of trees and shrubs in the form of circles on your diagram, so you'll know where the shade is greatest. Mark
steep erosion areas, spots that are swampy or low-lying, and rocky spots or other patches that will require special attention. Clearly identify items you'll want to conceal behind taller plants, such as a central air compressor or a utility box.

After you have represented the immovable items, save this as a template and make copies you can write on as you work out the locations for different plants. I suggest you use one copy to mark what you'll need to do in terms of soil preparation, as you work out how you plan to address each part of your property.

On a second copy of your area diagram, you can work out where you want to put each plant. This will help you prepare the soil, buy the plants, and begin to put them in the ground. Your template can also serve you well if you want to get the advice of a professional landscaper. You can save money on horticulturist visits to your yard by carrying an accurate representation of your garden spaces along with you.

WRITE DOWN YOUR PREFERENCES

Give yourself permission – and time – to consider what it is that you truly want. Now's the time to look at what you have, then turn your mind and imagination loose to decide what you want to do about it.

Here are four basic aspects of landscape planning that you will want to address:

1. What are the strengths and the weaknesses of your land? We've already addressed much of this issue when we took the lay of the land. Now it's time to review your findings and assess what you like about them, as well as what

you'd like to change. At this point, don't dwell on *how* you'll go about this; the purpose of this exercise is to clarify your hopes, yes, and your dreams for this property.

2. What existing plants, borders, and physical features do you want to keep the same? Which of these do you want to change or do away with?

3. What's your style? In other words, what kind of yard feels comfortable to you? Which infuses you with Life?   A natural-looking space? A well-balanced area with neatly displayed and well-maintained garden features?   What kind of area will you feel comfortable hanging out in?

4. What specific plants or features are your favorites for this space? As you read through the previous chapters, which plants, shrubs, grasses, or plant groupings stuck out to you as something you'd really like to have?

Make a note of these details so you can refer to them, even if you are not standing in your yard.

ISSUES

Here are some things to consider when you begin to plan out your gardening and landscaping:

- Do your proposed garden areas get at least six hours of sun per day?

- Where are the areas of partial or full shade?

- Does the soil drain well after it rains, or does it stay puddled for more than an hour?

- Where are the tree-covered areas, the spots where even grass finds it too shady to grow?

- What spots are so sunny that the grass fries to a crisp?

- What areas are so steep that rain tends to wash away all attempts at vegetation?

Each of these issues must be taken into account before you can move forward with your garden planning and soil preparation.

If you have a fully-shaded backyard, there is no way you can grow vegetables there; they would never get enough sunshine. In that case, perhaps a side or front yard would be a better alternative location for your vegetables. You can always plant shade-friendly foliage plants in the backyard. Tree cover makes for very nice shade gardens full of lush plants and ground cover.

Perhaps you have a swamp in your backyard. In that case you can either build up the soil or use raised beds if you want to establish a perennial garden there.

If your soil is less than perfect but drains well, there are many ways to improve it before you plant a garden. There are always ways to deal with intense sun, even to the point of putting up tents or artful shades in the garden to protect the plants – and you, whenever you venture out.

WHAT TO DO WITH THE OLD STUFF

Has your lilac bush seen better days? Is your park bench falling apart? Does your pond look like the swamp monster lives there? Has the statue of an angel lost its wings in a tussle with a tree branch? Are metal features twisted out of shape and covered with rust? Take note of these things; you just might be able to make use of them as your new garden takes shape.

Take inventory of your existing trees, shrubs, and flowers. They may be out of control or scraggly, but it may be possible to tame and incorporate them as part of your landscape. However, there's always a time to dig out the old and start afresh. It's largely up to you. You don't have to make these changes immediately, but eventually you'll need to decide what you can fix or repurpose and what you will need to dig out, cut down, and throw away.

Next, turn your attention to the inanimate objects in your yard. Maybe the pond could be refurbished with a little effort. That metal could be straightened, painted, and placed where it will set off your foliage displays. Or, it could be left to provide a contrasting statement in all its rustic glory. That park bench just might be solid enough to be nailed back together. That old gazing ball could, with a little polish or paint and a fresh pedestal, become a bright focal point.

STYLE

Two primary styles are available for landscaping your yard. The formal and informal styles are as different as night and day.

The informal style follows the natural flow of the property. Some yards may have straight, squared-off boundaries, but many will curve, ebb, and flow. The informal style follows those curves, creating soft edges of rounded beds with paths that meander throughout the plantings. There is little symmetry, but there is balance between plant placement and physical features in the garden.

The formal style is the complete opposite. It is very strict, with sharp right angles, tightly controlled hedges, straight paths, and symmetrical, geometric patterns. There is a place for everything and everything is in its place. Property lines are straight, with a house centered squarely on the property and symmetry ruling both garden and yard. A good example of this style would be the formal English garden.

DISPLAY

Your garden planning should allow your display to complement your house. If you have a country bungalow, a large formal garden would look out of character. It would feel much more comfortable with natural beds and softly defined borders. On the other hand, a modern angular home may look better with the formal style and border beds around the yard.

There are three types of display beds you can play with in either style of gardening.

BORDER BEDS

The border bed is set against some sort of structure like a wall or a fence. It includes focus plants with the taller plants standing in the back, against the structure they are bordering. Medium-sized plants are placed in front of the taller plants and short plants bring up the front of the bed. Border beds are rarely more than six feet wide so as to make even the plants in the back easy to reach. A good border bed can have ornamental grasses at the back with black-eyed Susans in front of them. It can proceed with blanket flowers and end with creeping thyme.

ISLAND BEDS

Island beds work well in the middle of a lawn or at the top of a drive where viewers can see around the entire bed. Taller plants grow in the center of this type of display, with medium-sized plants surrounding them and shorter plants approaching the end edge of the garden. For example, a dogwood tree in the center makes a great focal point, surrounded by hydrangea shrubs, with shasta daisies in front of them, and dianthus forming a border that marks the outer edge of the garden. This island of perennials is easily tended, since it can be approached from every direction. The varied blooming times of each plant guarantee a pop of color throughout the growing season.

NATURAL BEDS

A natural bed is so-called because it features plants that are native to your area and would likely be found there if the area was allowed to grow wild. Examples of natural beds – or naturescaping, as it is also called – include woodland gardens, prairie gardens, gardens alongside streams or ponds, and groundcover beds. A natural groundcover garden would be appropriate under a large tree. It could include local ivies and the type of groundcover that appears naturally in the area. Just take a walk in the woods near home and you'll see what serves as shady undergrowth in your area. A garden swing, a natural rock, or a birdbath can add a peaceful secondary focal point, or you can just enjoy the beauty of the unadulterated ground cover.

PLANT SELECTION

As you ponder which plants to use in your landscape and where to place them, there are a handful of characteristics to consider. The basic points to keep in mind are, environmental conditions, plant size, texture, shape, coloration, and when the plant blooms.

ENVIRONMENTAL CONDITIONS

Always locate together the plants that require similar growing conditions. Mix all the sun lovers together, but let all the shade plants reside in areas out of the reach of direct sun. Hostas and foxgloves go well together but don't try to put either one with roses, which require plenty of direct sunlight and different growing conditions.

You also want to check co-plant items that share similar soil conditions. Plant berries and azaleas together, because they thrive in acidic soil. You would never want to put a succulent that does not require large amounts of water near a hydrangea that does. Keep your Mediterranean herbs away from plants that need a great deal of water, but plant them near that sedum and they will both be happy.

PLANT SIZE

You'll want to take into consideration the size of your perennials when full-grown. Avoid placing tall plants so that they shade shorter ones, especially when the short plants require full sun exposure. Placing a really tiny plant next to a huge one can look pretty silly, but it isn't just the height you need to consider. It is also the spread of the plant. Some mature plants will require 15 to 20 inches of space to spread, so consider this when you are planning your layout. Always consider the mature size of the plant instead of the actual size of the plant you will be placing in the ground. What size will it be in two to five years?

TEXTURE

Different plants have different textures. Some have coarse leaves while others' are fine and delicate. Some leaves are smooth while others are bumpy or fuzzy. Iris have large, flat leaves that could be considered coarse while ferns have lacy fine foliage. It's important to vary the texture in your garden. You don't want one plant to take over the whole area. You want all the plants to work together to provide a pleasing textural variety in addition to color and size variation.

SHAPE

The shape of a plant also contributes to the beauty and appeal of the whole garden. Any garden bed needs a balance between order and variety. Consider offsetting the vertical growth of ornamental grasses, daisies, black-eyed Susans, and lilies with mounding plants like silver mount or blue fescue. Contrast these with spreading plants like lavender or dianthus and creeping flowers and herbs like thyme or pachysandra to create a delightful garden.

COLOR

While you are busy creating variety in size and texture, don't forget the power of color to draw the eye. You can create a focal point by using all pink and purple, an all-white garden with varying textures and heights of blooms, a bi-colored mix like yellow and blue, or perhaps you prefer a profusion of colors running riot throughout.

BLOOM SEQUENCE

You will probably prefer not to have all your flowers bloom at once. Instead, you can arrange for flowers to bloom in a sequence that gives your garden color throughout the growing season. Tulips, crocus, daffodils and hyacinths generally bloom first in the spring. These can give way to shasta daisies, coneflower and hosta in the summer and then yield to colorful chrysanthemum puffs in the fall. You can plan your garden so that there is always something blooming during the growing season.

THEME GARDENS

Many people opt for a theme garden to simplify the myriad choices and contribute a cohesive and beautiful look to their landscape. Here are some themes you can adopt for your garden.

Rustic/Countryside/Cottage Garden – Mass plantings of colorful blooms with contrasting shapes, textures and colors make for a less formal but profusion of life. Most of the perennials have long bloom times and beds are full but not crowded.

Butterfly Garden – Certain flowers and shrubs attract colorful butterflies to the area. The most well-known are the butterfly bush, coneflowers, lemon balm, thyme, and salvias. Anything trumpet-shaped or in the red, pink, or purple color range will attract butterflies. It doesn't hurt to plant some honeysuckle up a trellis and place a large stone in a bird bath to give butterflies a place to light and drink.

Prairie Garden – A prairie garden is full of the area's wildflowers, scattered and intermingled with ornamental grasses. This is another form of naturescape, where you use plants that naturally thrive in your locale.

Ground-cover Shade Garden – Plant grasses and ferns around trees and opt for shade-loving perennials that grow at varying heights with different textures and colors. You can plant 50 to 100 of the same species as groundcover.

I hope this has piqued your curiosity and sparked ideas for your own perennial garden. The possibilities are endless. Just look around you. No two gardens are alike. You can also get ideas from what your neighbors are doing and take notes of the landscaping whenever you are out and about.

When you go to purchase your plants, take advantage of the expertise of the individuals who work with those plants. Most plant stores are more than happy to share tips on successful planting and care. For that very reason, I prefer to buy from greenhouses and smaller businesses that specialize in plants and/or landscaping.

Chapter 8: Potted Perennials

Although perennials do best in the ground, some perform well in pots or boxes. This can be a godsend if you have limited to no growing space. Even an apartment balcony or windowsill can become home to healthy perennials If you have physical limitations that make it impossible to tend a traditional garden, you can always surround yourself with a variety of perennials in pots or in a raised bed. Some gardeners prefer to accentuate their front porch or entryway with live plants. Others like to punctuate the natural look of their back deck, bringing the backyard garden that much closer with potted varieties scattered about. You can use potted plants to complement an existing garden or to make a solo statement with bright color next to your door. You can also soften the look of a concrete walkway or stairs by dotting them every so often with potted varieties.

ADVANTAGES TO PLANTING PERENNIALS IN CONTAINERS

Planting perennials in pots gives gardeners a jumpstart on the growing season. The pot is is easily moved around to sheltered areas if the weather gets rough. If a pot is big and heavy, you can easily purchase a wheeled dolly that will fit inconspicuously beneath the pot; the wheels allow you to easily move your pot around, both to take advantage of changing sunlight and to accommodate weather conditions.

Container planting allows northern gardeners to grow plants they may not otherwise be able to enjoy; the plants can be set outside to benefit from the sunshine and fresh air, then brought inside to brighten the house and freshen the air when cold weather sets in.

If you have perennials that require a lot of sun, potting them will make it easier for you to move them to follow the sun. A pot can also make it possible to grow plants that require soil that is vastly different from the soil in your yard.

DISADVANTAGES

While there are many advantages to planting perennials in containers, there are also a few drawbacks. One is that water evaporates quicker when a plant is in a pot. Air circulates around a clay pot, allowing it to dry faster than the same soil would dry if in the ground. Therefore, potted plants will require more watering, just to keep up with the evaporation. This is even more accentuated when the weather is warm and windy.

Plants in a pot cannot reach down deep with their roots to draw nutrients and minerals from the earth. It's up to you, the gardener to regularly replenish the soil with nutrients in the form of supplemental fertilizer. When planting in containers, it is adviseable to not apply fertilizer right away. Instead, wait a month, then use a liquid fertilizer suited to the plant in the pot. After that, fertilize every three to four weeks during the growing period and stop until a month before the plant comes out of dormancy.

A major challenge, probably the biggest, is overwintering. When plants are in the ground, they have natural defenses against the cold. When they are in a pot, their roots are not as protected by the earth. They are above ground and extra protection is needed so they don't freeze and the plant will revive in the spring. There are several ways to go about protecting plants in pots. Sink the pots into the ground by digging a hole deep enough so that the pot lip is all that is left above ground. Once spring comes around, the pot is removed and cleaned up. Another way to protect pots is to put them in an area where wind and snow won't be a problem. A garage with a window or enclosed breezeway will protect them enough. Just make sure that the pots don't totally dry out. Avoid adding water that will freeze the roots when it is really cold. The last way to insulate a flower pot is to coil chicken wire around the pot that does not touch the pot. Place dry leaves, pine needles or bark mulch in the space between the pot and chicken wire all the way up and over the top of the pot. Wrap the outside of the chicken wire with burlap or another material that will keep wind out.

SOIL

Any commercial potting soil will do. If the particular plant in the pot needs a more acidic soil (do a pH test before you do anything else) If need be, add garden sulfur or aluminum sulphate. If the soil needs to be more alkaline, add agricultural lime. You don't have to add much to a pot. Check with your garden center if you are not sure how much to add.

PLANTS

Smaller, more compact plants do a little better in containers, but if the container is big enough, tall plants like coneflower or foxglove can make their home in pots. The following plants do very well in containers. Plant them as a specimen plant with only one kind in a pot, or mix them up placing the tallest plant in the center, mid-size plants around that and lower or cascading perennials on the edge. Don't restrict your plant pallate to only the plants below. These are just the ones that have proven to do well in containers.

Aster	Astilbe	Bergenia	Black Eyed Susan
Calendula	Chrysanthemum	Clematis	Coneflower
Coral Bells	Coreopsis	Day Lilies	Dianthus
Ferns	Forget-Me-Nots	Hellebore	Hosta
Iris (Japanese)	Iris (Siberian)	Lady's Mantle	Lavender
Lemon Balm	Mint	Sage	Sedge
Thyme	Yarrow		

Any of the spring flowering bulbs are suitable for pots, like tulips, crocous, hyacinth and dafoldil. Avoid planting tall grasses or large fruit bushes in containers. Be careful of those perennials with

101

long taproots as they may need more room than a container can give.

HOW TO PLANT PERENNIALS IN POTS

Plant perennials the same way you would plant any flower in a container:

1. Clean containers out with a half bleach and half water solution. Rinse well and let dry.

2. Make sure there a drain hole in the bottom of the container. If it is large, place some screen or a coffee filter flat over it. This allows water to drain, but the soil will stay in.

3. If you are using a large pot, place a one inch layer of fine gravel in the bottom of the pot to facilitate drainage better.

4. Fill the pot with soil about ¾ full, place the roots or bulb of the plant in and fill the pot to within 1-inch of the rim. The container plant being planted should be at the same level as it was in the original pot.

5. Always leave at least one inch so that water remains in the pot when watering and doesn't spill out.

6. Press down on the soil to get rid of any air pockets around the roots.

7. Water the plant and wait until it drains. If the soil sinks more than one or two inches, add a little more.

8. Those perennials that need to be moist will get an advantage if you place a little mulch at the top of the pot. It will retain moisture and keep roots cool.

Watch for indications that the plant needs fertilizer. This is indicated by a general yellowing of the leaves. Also make sure to water frequently. After a year or two, the roots may become pot bound. The roots will grow continually with perennials and they may wind around and around inside of the pot. Sometimes you will see the roots break through the surface of the soil. The pot may break open in severe cases or the plant will stop growing and not do very well. When a plant becomes pot bound, you must replant it in a bigger pot.

Go ahead and plant your perennials in pots. Plant them alone, plant them with other perennials or add a few annuals for some variety. Your perennials should come back year after year if you heed precautions for overwintering in cold areas.

Chapter 9: The Therapeutic Perennial Garden

Therapeutic gardens are usually outdoor areas designed to boost an individual's physical, psychological, and spiritual well-being. Many hospitals, nursing homes, and retirement centers now boast therapeutic gardens as part of their amenities. The hospital near me has a beautiful outdoor area full of soothing flowers and a refreshing variety of plants, as well as a small fish pond. It provides comfortable outdoor seating and an open space where patients and their families can relax in the fresh air and restful quiet. Although these therapeutic gardens are usually created by a team of architects, designers, and professional gardeners, you can easily build your own soothing and inspiring therapeutic garden right in your own backyard.

Research shows that people who spend time outdoors, surrounded by nature, are more likely to experience positive emotions and they have a greater sense of well-being. Therapeutic gardens generally include popular, native, nontoxic flowers and vegetables with ornamental plants that thrive in natural light and varying amounts of shade. They often include elements such as a patio, smooth walkways, comfortable seating, adequate evening lighting, a fountain or pond, and shady spots like an umbrella or gazebo. The majority of perennials in a therapeutic garden are attractive to friendly creatures, like hummingbirds, butterflies, and finches.

The size of a therapeutic garden is irrelevant; all you require is a space that encourages you to relax and escape for a while. Your first step is to imagine what your garden will look like. There is no right or wrong way to make a therapeutic garden, so you can be as creative as you'd like. If it helps, you can give your garden a color scheme or plan it around your favorite features, like a park bench, a relaxing chair, or a small water feature. You're only limited by your imagination...well, and your budget. Even then, with ingenuity, you'd be amazed at how inexpensively you can turn your vision into reality.

The next step is to figure out the "basics" of your garden. Just as you did with designing your yard, it is helpful to map out your garden space on a piece of paper and then mark out space for each plant you want to include. This helps you provide space for distinctive features such as hedges, borders, water systems, and furniture.

In this step, it is important to consider the sound levels of your therapeutic garden. A quiet garden in the city, may well involve putting up a privacy fence or using plants to muffle the sound. If you intend to incorporate peaceful and relaxing music into your garden, you'll want to plan the best locations for speakers and decide how you will conceal your sound system. Take into account the terrain of your proposed garden space, letting the natural contours of the ground suggest pathways and specific plant features.

You can research therapeutic gardening to get more ideas. I recommend you keep your original garden layout template in a place where you can copy it and make changes as you get more ideas. Keep a file with pictures of anything that gives you inspiration. Even after you've built your garden, hold onto these ideas; over time you may wish to make changes and experiment with additional plants to enhance the therapeutic experience.

Next, consider the overall surface of your garden paths. This can make a huge difference in what is relaxing to you. Some people prefer grass, while others may prefer bricks or concrete pavement. Some people even use mosaics as the path surface, although this can be time-consuming. It is best to pick whatever is best-suited for you.

Consider also any physical structures in your garden. If you want to include artwork and statues, I recommend reaching out to local artists to see what is available. By supporting an artist in your area, you can add to your "feel-good" attitude while helping out someone at the same time. Again, whatever structures you choose to include – artwork, rocks, water – depends on your personal preference.

Another item to consider is the possibility of using raised beds. It is much easier to manage a variety of plants in raised beds, and it is much easier to maintain the beds themselves. Potting soil or mixtures including potting soil make it easy to keep the soil aerated and sustain a healthy place for plants to grow. It also makes the garden much easier to maintain and, should you decide to include statues or other decorative objects, they will be raised up and more easily seen.

Some therapeutic gardens have a specific activity in mind. An exercise garden can include a chinning bar or a flat surface covered with outdoor carpeting on which to do ground work. You can include a labyrinth as part of your garden, where you can walk the path to enlightenment. You may prefer a pergola with a cozy chair to read in or a lightly splashing fountain to add to the restorative, refreshing quality of your garden.

Finally, and most importantly, you will decide which perennials to plant in your garden. One of the easiest therapeutic gardens is a sensory garden where you choose plants that appeal to all five senses. If you're a hands-on person, you may find it helpful to include plants with distinct textures. If you're more stimulated by taste, you might find it appealing to include fruit and vegetable perennials.   If you're most relaxed by sight, you can plant perennials that flower in your favorite colors or bushes that attract butterflies. If you're soothed by sounds, you may consider using plants that attract songbirds along with the soft splash of a fountain. If you are affected by aromas, include plants that give off a distinct, pleasant fragrance. The following are plants that appeal to each of the five senses. Intermingle these perennials so that you find something to entice each sense in every corner of the garden.

TOUCH

- Allium – the globes look solid but they aren't.

- Clematis – have anthers that look like fireworks and you just want to touch them.

- Lamb's ear – soft and velvety silvery green leaves that look like...lambs' ears.

- Sedum – looks like soft clouds of flowers.

- Ornamental Grasses – most grasses have wispy ends that look and feel very soft.

- Pussywillows – this shrub produces fuzzy little catkins in the spring that are as soft as kitten fur.

- Roses often have velvety petals; just watch out for the thorns.

TASTE

- Lemon Balm – tastes much like its namesake.

- Sage – strong earthy flavor, reminiscent of sausage.

- Blueberries, currants, strawberries – these plants do not have thorns and are safe to grow in a therapeutic garden; besides, the fruits taste good.

- Mint – chew a leaf for fresh breath and digestive benefits.

- Honeysuckle – If you pull out the stamen and suck on the bottom of the flower, it tastes like honey.

- Any vegetable that comes back year after year like asparagus or Jerusalem artichoke can be chewed on.

SIGHT

- Black-eyed Susan – related to the sunflower and similar to daisies, the vivid color will spice up any garden.

- Coneflower – also known as Echinacea, these flowers are pleasing to the eyes and are often used medicinally.

- Clematis – A flowering vine, this perennial produces delicate colorful blooms.

- Heather – aromatic as well as pleasing to the eyes.

- Coreopsis – Bright and colorful flowers that invite you to cut and add them to bouquets.

- Asters – Great for adding color to your autumn garden.

- Astilbe – Provides splashes of vivid hues to shady nooks.

- Statuary, rocks, water features, and breeze-powered mobiles can provide focal points for meditation or just for resting the eyes.

SOUND

- Ornamental grasses – their rustling can be very relaxing.

- Butterfly bush – will attract hummingbirds as well as butterflies.

- Honeysuckle, yarrow, shasta daisies, coneflowers, and black-eyed Susans draw in buzzing insects and birds.

- Audible objects like wind chimes, rain sticks, fountains, or waterfalls add refreshing ambiance.

SMELL

- Roses, especially the older varieties, bring wonderful scents to the garden.

- Lilac – a bush with a distinct fragrance.

- Fennel – with lacy, bright green leaves, this plant smells like anise or licorice.

- Lavender has a strong scent that is clean and pleasant.

- Any strong-smelling herb like mint or lemon balm.

- Nicotiana has a very strong scent as does honeysuckle. It is often possible to catch a whiff from across the yard.

- Iris flowers have a strong scent, as do some daylily varieties.

WHAT ELSE TO INCLUDE?

Aside from flowers, bushes, and shrubs, there are many other things you can include in a therapeutic garden. Whatever you decide to add in is completely up to you, making it your own personal space. One idea is to give your therapeutic garden a theme. For example, my grandmother is passionate about nautical décor, so she ended up buying a customized lighthouse with working solar lighting to add to her garden. I've also seen people complement their gardens with seashells, a replica steering wheel, portholes, fishermen, and statues. I've even seen a salvaged boat and a bed frame incorporated into a garden!

INVITATION TO DREAM

I recommend you choose a theme for the place where you escape, relax, and surround yourself with your passions. Try sitting quietly in the spot, pen and paper at hand, and daydreaming about your favorite things. What are the things that bring restful calm into your life? What leaves you feeling refreshed? What things help you detach from the details of your life and set you free simply to be?

After you have fixed an image of these things in your mind, imagine how you could go about incorporating at least one in your therapeutic garden. If nothing else, the creative exercise alone will be therapeutic, because it gives you an excuse to think about the things that breathe life into your soul. I recommend doing this every so often, giving yourself permission to think of ways to enhance the healing nature of your therapeutic garden and then, as an act of caring for yourself, finding ways to include these ideas as part of your personal garden spot.

Chapter 10: Basic Principles of Perennial Care And Maintenance

It's easy to feel overwhelmed, as you read the individual descriptions of what each plant requires. You may wonder if you'll ever get a handle on how deep to plant them, which plant to prune in the spring, versus which require cutting back in the fall, when to fertilize and mulch, and the seemingly myriad variables involved in maintaining each plant.

This chapter will, hopefully, simplify the process somewhat by providing basic guidelines that hold true for most perennials. While each individual plant, it is true, has its own personality with characteristics and needs to match, there are some basic principles you can adopt that will make it easier, overall, to successfully care for each type of perennial in your garden.

RECOMMENDED TOOLS

First off, let's talk about some of the basic tools you'll need, with a few guidelines for using them.

- Sharp scissors or hand pruner. You'll need these to to deadhead spent blooms, prevent some blooms from going to seed, or cut away dead wood.

- Trowel. A hand-trowel will allow you to provide planting holes for young starts. You can use it to mix in nutrients with the soil and to work in tight spaces between plants.

- Hose/sprinkler/soaker hose. Unless your plants are completely indigenous to your locale, you'll need to occasionally provide water to keep them healthy and growing. At the very least, you'll need a hose and a good thumb for spraying the water about. If your thumb gets tired, I'd also recommend a spray nozzle that will allow you to gently water fresh sprouts and extend the reach of the spray well into your garden.

You'll want to use a sprinkler if you need to cover a wide area with moisture; otherwise you'd be spending a lot of time just standing in your garden, holding a hose.

Use soaker hoses to water your garden when possible; they get water to the root of the issue, literally, and do this much more effectively than sprinklers. A soaker hose can be a godsend when you're starting new plants; it provides continuous moisture directly to the soil, helping to establish an ideal environment for young sprouts. The soaker hose gets the water to precisely where it's needed and it minimizes the loss of moisture via evaporation.

Sprinklers deposit droplets of water indiscriminately, on leaves and ground alike. This can be fine, if the leaves are not prone to water spots, mildew, or fungus. If you *do* use a sprinkler, don't water late in the day; if water stays on the leaves and stems overnight, there is greater chance for disease to set in. I recommend early morning watering, if you're using a sprinkler. You will avoid the dangers of late afternoon watering and you will lose less moisture to evaporation, if you water in the morning.

- Garden spade with flat edge to help disengage weeds.

- Lawn rake to rake up debris gently and to spread light ground cover.

- Steel rake for spreading mulch or smoothing soil

- Fertilizer designed for perennials.

- Mulch – wood bark, pine boughs, needles, leaves.

- Loppers are only necessary if you are dealing with bushes that grow branches thicker than a pencil. However, if you work with forsythia, lilacs, or even some roses, you will find them an indispensable tool for removing dead wood, thinning bushes, and training branches away from walls or fences

OBSERVATION

Inspect your plants weekly. A casual walk around your garden will give you a good indication of the health of your plants. Look for holes in leaves or ragged edges that have been chewed on. Look for spotted leaves that should not have spots and brown leaves that should be green. If you aren't sure what is afflicting a plant, take a leaf or flower to your local garden center.

Pull weeds; they compete for nutrients and moisture with your plants. Notice thick areas that are in need of thinning, to keep the patch healthy, Look around for spots that would serve well as locations for the thinned plants.

FOOD AND WATER

Fertilize and mulch perennials as needed. Herbs rarely need fertilization but flowers, shrubs, and fruit bushes may require it occasionally. Fertilize early in the spring, using a granular, slow release fertilizer designed for perennials. Scratch it into the soil near the plant and water the area. It is also possible to fertilize with water-soluble perennial fertilizer.

Some perennials only need one shot of fertilizer in the spring, while others may need to be fertilized every month or so. Mulch the roots of perennials to keep moisture in and to keep the roots from drying out too fast. This also keeps the roots cool in summer and warm in winter. A three or four-inch layer of mulch is acceptable.

RESTRAINING AND TRAINING

113

Pinch off the flowers of leafy perennials to keep them from going to seed. This is important for any fall-blooming plants you want to flower. Keep pinching them back until August and then let them bloom freely.

Stake tall perennials like tomatoes, coneflower, and foxglove. This will protect them from breakage in wind or heavy rain. Always place your stakes early in the spring so the roots will grow around it and not be damaged or disturbed later.

Divide perennials when necessary. Usually a perennial will need to be divided every three to four years. You will be able to tell because it will not grow as aggressively as usual.

While you can divide your plants at any time during the growing season, it is best to divide them in either the spring or fall, when the cooler weather will present less of a shock to the disturbed roots. To ease the process, give the soil a good watering a couple days before you dig up the roots to divide them.

FALL PREPARATION

Protect perennials in colder regions well before the ground freezes. Place a four- to six-inch layer of mulch on the ground around your plants.

- **Grasses** – After your grasses have turned brown, you can cut them back to within eight inches of the ground.

- **Bulbs** – Let plants that grow from bulbs die back completely before cutting away the dried material. These plants need to absorb all the energy from the leaves into their root bulbs to prepare for a strong growth the next year.

- **Shrubs** that bloom before they start new growth in the spring, should be pruned back in the fall.

- **Mulch** can help your plants weather the cold. I have found pine boughs to be the best defenses against ice and snow. Bark mulch and dry leaves also help.

-

SPRING CARE

- You'll want to rake away the mulch in the spring, to facilitate the sun warming the soil and to make it easier for the plants to emerge from the ground.

- Add compost every spring in a two- to three-inch layer around the roots of your plants to add nutrients to the soil.

WHEN TO PRUNE

When in doubt, don't prune. Plants grow just fine without pruning; the practice is just needed when you have a plant that is growing too large for the space where it lives. If it threatens to dominate or grow over other plants in the area, you will need to prune it back. If a plant grows too tall for your liking, you'll want to judiciously cut back some of the larger branch stems further back toward the core of the bush, to allow for new growth to appear at a lower level than before.

To be safe, don't prune a shrub until *after* it has finished blooming. Some bushes bloom on old wood; this means they produce flowers, like the forsythia does, before they set on leaves in the spring. If you prune this plant before the leaves appear, you'll be cutting off your blooms for that year. Fortunately, the plant itself will not be harmed; you'll just lose your chance to enjoy the fragrant color until next year.

Most shrubs that flower on new wood can be pruned in early spring, as soon as buds set on, so you can see which branches are still alive and growing. They won't be harmed by pruning during the growing season, for the most part. For both types of shrub, you can prune back dead wood at any time, to make room for healthy new growth. If you're unsure what type of shrub you have, watch it for a year; your bush won't bloom any better or worse if you don't prune it for a year.

A little attention paid to your perennials can extend their life by years. These plants are an investment well worth protecting, because they increase the attractiveness of your home even as they fulfill the need for beauty and refreshing surroundings.

Chapter 11: Bonus Chapter – Bringing Perennials Indoors

Indoor plants are usually tropical evergreens that are unable to survive outdoors. They aren't really considered perennials, but since they last all year round inside, we can give them honorary perennial status. Indoor perennials give your home a taste of nature and add to its beauty. They promote clean indoor air by processing carbon dioxide and converting it to oxygen. Indoor plants can add a peaceful quality to a living space.

Indoor perennials will need the same care as outdoor plants. Most indoor perennials require low to medium sun exposure. This is easily provided by placement near a window. They require high humidity levels, proper soil moisture, and regular fertilization, usually every four to six months. In this chapter, you will discover some key indoor perennials and learn their individual care needs.

ALOE VERA

There are more than 200 varieties of Aloe worldwide but the most popular type is the aloe vera plant. The aloe vera is a tropical succulent plant that cannot grow outdoors in cold zones. However, they make for great indoor plants when you provide the right conditions.

Place your aloe vera in a spot where it receives a good amount of sunlight. Wait until the soil becomes completely dry before watering it with one to two cups of water. During the summer, you can actually keep it outside. In the summer, you'll want to soak the soil with water completely, but allow it to dry completely before watering again.

If you decide to repot an aloe vera plant, use a container that is wide rather than deep, because of the plant's shallow roots. You can use cactus soil mix or a combination of potting soil, perlite, and coarse sand. The aloe vera can be propagated by seed or, more easily, by using offsets that grow around their base. You can fertilize your Aloe vera with half-strength bloom fertilizer, once a year, in the spring.

The nectar in the Aloe vera plants may attract hummingbirds. The plant's "leaves" contain a thick gel that can promote the healing of sunburn, cuts, burns and rashes.

CHINESE EVERGREENS

Chinese evergreens are hybrid plants of the Aroid family, a group of subtropical plants from Southeast Asia. Chinese evergreens are known for being highly adaptable. They thrive in less-than-optimum lighting conditions and do not require much moisture, making them easy to grow and maintain. However, they do not fare well in cold temperatures.

The Chinese evergreen requires temperatures above 55 degrees Fahrenheit. It is so sensitive to the cold that patches and spots will form on their leaves if exposed to cold air. This plant will not survive in any temperature below 55 degrees.

Chinese evergreens bear large, pointed, variegated green leaves with a smooth texture. Their leaves grow between six and 10 inches long and up to three inches wide. These plants may produce small flowers with poisonous red berries in the summer. The entire plant grows to a maximum height of three feet and older leaves tend to fall off as the plant ages.

Chinese evergreens prefer low sunlight exposure. Too much sunlight causes the leaves to fade. You will want to plant it in a high-quality potting mix that promotes a consistent, moisture level. Of course, its moist soil will be sustained by regular watering. These plants prefer the low humidity levels typically found inside the house. During the spring and the summer, you'll want to fertilize your plant monthly. You'll know it's time to find a larger pot when your Chinese evergreen outgrows its existing home. The plant is propagated through stem cuttings or root division.

CYCLAMEN

Cyclamen are tropical plants that will live for a long time, as long as you provide the right care and proper growing conditions. They grow in beautifully bright colors that will perk up any home. The cyclamen prefers an environment where the temperature does not drop below 40 degrees Fahrenheit or rise above 68 degrees.

Cyclamen are sensitive to over- and under-watering, so it is important to ensure your pots have proper drainage. Determine when you need to water cyclamen by examining its soil. If the soil is dry, give it some water. Also look out for drooping leaves, a sure sign of under-watering. It is important to water the roots directly and avoid getting any water on the stems or leaves. Fertilize cyclamen once a month using a half-strength water-soluble fertilizer.

After a cyclamen plant blooms, it will enter a dormant phase in which it will appear as if the plant is dying. When this occurs, stop watering it at once and move the plant into a dark, cool area for two months. Remove any dead leaves and just let it be. After two months, begin to water the plant again, soaking the soil completely. If the pot seems crowded at this point, re-pot it into a larger container. Once the leaves begin to grow again, you can return to its normal care regimen.

FERNS

Ferns are perennials with uniquely-textured, fine foliage. They grow well in moist, shaded conditions. There are many sub-varieties of fern with interesting features. Some ferns are considered evergreens, while others die in the fall and return in the spring.

Ferns require partial shade and well-drained soil. Too much sunlight scorches their leaves. Ferns grow to between one and six feet tall and most spread their fronds wide, so be careful to allow them room to grow. It is important to keep ferns well-watered.

GERBER DAISY

Gerber daisies produce brightly colored pink, white, orange or yellow flowers that will grab anyone's attention. Their stems are short but their blooms are profuse and long-lasting. These daisies are commonly grown as outdoor perennials in mild climates, but you can also grow and maintain them inside your home year-round. Many people throw the plants away after one year, but if you provide the right conditions, you can sustain a Gerber daisy for at least three years. The plant is easy to care for; as long as they get the right amount of sun, the rest of their care is minimal.

Admittedly, the lighting requirements for Gerber daisies are a little tricky. While they generally thrive in bright light and medium temperatures, too much sunlight can kill their leaves and too little sunlight can prevent them from blooming. The best solution: place them where they get three to five hours of direct morning sunlight but are shaded from the strong afternoon sun.

Gerber daisies do best when the temperature hovers around 70 degrees Fahrenheit, but can tolerate cooler indoor temperatures. The plant grows best in sandy soil. Water deeply when the soil feels dry. During the winter, water Gerber daisies less frequently. Apply fertilizer during the growing season, between March and August.

Trim dead flowers to encourage additional blooms. Discard diseased or damaged leaves. If the Gerber daisy grows too much for its original pot, replant it into a bigger container.

GOLDEN POTHOS

Golden pothos are popular and easy to maintain. Originally found in the Solomon Islands, the golden pothos is known for its long stems and green and glazed heart-shaped leaves that hold a tint of yellow. These plants grow well in hanging baskets since their stems tend to trail down.

The golden pothos requires bright but indirect sunlight. Direct sunlight can be hard on the leaves. It grows best in rich, well-drained potting soil and requires a minimum indoor temperature of 55 degrees Fahrenheit.

It is best to keep a golden pothos watered consistently throughout the summer. but you can cut back during the winter. The plant prefers moist soil. Apply a time-release fertilizer at the start of the growing season or alternatively use a liquid fertilizer. Reduce fertilization during the winter.

You can propagate the golden pothos with cuttings rooted in water. Since the vines can quickly overtake the container, repotting is usually a common activity. The best time to repot this plant is during the spring. If you prefer, you can set stakes in the pot to encourage the vines to climb.

PEACE LILY

Peace lilies are popular tropical perennial houseplants that can bring many benefits to your home. Peace lilies, which are part of the aroid family, have pointed, oval-shaped leaves with a glossy texture. White flowers will eventually bloom. NASA has classified peace lilies as one of the top 10 houseplants for cleaning the air in your home. They are relatively easy to care for and easy to propagate.

Peace lilies grow between two feet and 40 inches tall. White flowers often appear in the spring. The better you care for a peace lily, the more likely it is to bloom in the fall as well. This plant can be repotted easily once their roots begin to appear. It is recommended to repot the peace lily every one to two years.

Peace lilies prefer shade and only require indirect, moderate sunlight throughout the day. Golden leaves are a sign that your lily is getting too much sunlight. Brown spots on the leaves occur when sunlight has scorched the plant. The ideal temperature ranges between 65 and 80 degrees Fahrenheit, which makes it easy to care for indoors. A drop to 45 degrees can kill the plant, so keep it away from drafts in winter.

Plant your peace lilies in potting soil that is rich, loose, and full of organic matter. While fertilization is not required, you can use a basic houseplant fertilizer once a month during the summer to boost blooming. You can tell when a peace lily needs water because the leaves will droop, indicating that it's thirsty. You'll, generally need to water a peace lily once a week. In addition, you should spray it weekly with a mist of distilled water. It will need less water during the winter. Even if you forget to water a peace lily and it looks completely dead, water and mist just might revive it.

SPIDER PLANTS

Spider plants are the most common type of hanging indoor perennial and they are best known for their ease of growing. Native to South Africa, mature spider plants grow long arching leaves. Its offshoots look like a set of spider legs, hence the name. It also produces small white flowers.

To propagate a spider plant, simply plant the offshoot "spiders" into a pot once they have developed roots. Seedlings will mature within two years. Divide matured plants during your repotting process, although spider plants do not require annual repotting.

Spider plants are not picky about sunlight. They thrive best in bright indirect light. A little direct sunlight will not hurt the plant; it will grow well in partial shade. During summer months be liberal with watering and add in an occasional misting. However, you should cut back on watering during the winter.

It is important to keep spider plants in temperatures that are above 50 degrees Fahrenheit. Temperatures below 50 degrees can be fatal. Spider plants prefer potting mix that is aerated and will drain quickly. It is best to fertilize spider plants with either fertilizer pellets or liquid fertilizer, but only at the beginning of the summer.

SNAKE PLANT

The snake plant, also known as the mother-in-law tongue, is a mildly poisonous perennial originally from South Africa. These plants have thick vertical leaves that stand upright from the pot. The leaves are dark green; some have lighter variations and at least one variety rims its leaves with a yellow border. The leaves can make your pets sick, if they chew on the leaves.

Snake plants grow up to 48 inches tall. They prefer bright, indirect sunlight but are capable of growing in limited light conditions. The plant grows best in temperatures that range between 60 and 85 degrees Fahrenheit. It also prefers slightly moist soil with great drainage. You can propagate it via plant division or by cutting the leaves.

Fertilize your snake plant once a month with a nitrate-free fertilizer during the summer only. You do not need to fertilize these plants in the winter. If the leaves begin to droop, it is a sign that they are not receiving enough water. Don't repot this type of plant unless absolutely necessary; it does best when left undisturbed.

Conclusion

I hope this book was able to help you to discover all of the wonderful benefits of planting perennials. Now that you have seen the various forms perennials can take, you are equipped to choose precisely the types of plants that will serve you best.

Perennials can open up a world of possibilities in your garden. From soil-hugging ground cover, to lofty swaying grasses, you are sure to find the right plant to meet the need of the moment. Regardless of your climate or the makeup of your soil, you will have a variety of colors, shapes, and sizes of plants from which to choose and enhance your property.

The next step is to plan your garden. Go back over the planning instructions in Chapter 7. You'll want to survey your landscape and determine the specific needs or challenges presented by each area of your yard.

After you decide what areas to modify and which to work with as is, you'll want to decide on the structure of each garden area. Review Chapters 2 through 6 to choose specific plant groupings that will grow well in that area and will complement each other, providing variety and contrast in color, shape, size, and texture.

Then, select your gardening tools from the information in Chapter 10 and get started!

Remember, by nurturing perennials, you are investing in your future. With each plant you set in the ground, you are building a healthy environment for vibrant living. You are caring for yourself and are creating a legacy for those who come after you. So have some fun and see what type of paradise you can create.

Thanks for reading.

If this book helped you or someone you know in any way, then please spare a few moments right now to leave a nice review.

My Other Books

Be sure to check out my author page at:
https://www.amazon.com/author/susanhollister

UK: http://amzn.to/2qiEzA9

Or simply type my name into the search bar: Susan Hollister

Thank You

Made in the USA
Lexington, KY
20 January 2018